'*Drifts* invites us to see the world differently, as if through a kaleidoscope for the first time. Natasha Burge's evocative prose spins out mental waterfalls, sand drifts and snowdrifts, and seas where ancient myths come to life. Her tales will sidle up to you, nudge you, search you, surprise you. In a world powered by neurodiversity, our private and public geographies are revealed to be a chaotic patchwork whose colours harmonize through creativity and love. *Drifts* is a stunning achievement.'

Hassan Melehy, author of *Kerouac: Language, Poetics, and Territory*

'This is wonderful – a wonderful everywhere and everything book where we encounter not only the Gulf War and the falling Twin Towers of Manhattan but also London, Bahrain, Texas, Dhahran, souqs, sandstorms, slantways Arabic, and cats with weeping eyes. Read on. Drift on.'

John Schad, author of *Paris Bride: A Modernist Life*

Drifts

Drifts

Natasha Burge

First published in 2023 by
Footnote Press

www.footnotepress.com

Footnote Press Limited
4th Floor, Victoria House, Bloomsbury Square, London WC1B 4DA

Distributed by Bonnier Books UK, a division of Bonnier Books
Sveavägen 56, Stockholm, Sweden

First printing
1 3 5 7 9 10 8 6 4 2

A CIP catalogue record for this book is available from
the British Library and the Library of Congress

ISBN (paperback): 978-1-804-44010-0
ISBN (ebook): 978-1-804-44011-7

Book designed and typeset by VictoriaHeathSilk.com
Printed and bound in Great Britain
by Clays Ltd, Elcograf S.p.A.

To Cody and Polly

Drifts emerges from the interstices.
It intends to tell a truthful story, though not always an
entirely factual one. Dates, names, and details of places,
events, and people have occasionally been altered, invented,
or unabashedly embellished. Throughout *Drifts* Arabic words
are used and, in order to make the text itself a site
of transculturality, they are not italicized.

'Earth's crammed with heaven'

– Elizabeth Barrett Browning

1.

An editor suggests I write about being an alien. This word I like, with its superabundance of meaning. It reminds me of visa stamps crowding an already full passport, of space shuttles and stardust and solitude. Of finding strange meaning in the storied landscape. It rings true.

I tell her about skoliogeography, my new secret something. Skolio, from the Greek word for crooked, and geography, literally meaning earth writing – a crooked psychogeography yearning toward transcendence in the drift away from center. It rings truer.

She asks if I could write about this theory's development; she wants to know how it came to be. Trajectories, she mentions, timelines, something linear and explanatory.

But it is not a theory, I explain, but a space to seek the marvelous, indeed, even the miraculous, in the mundane. Wherever I position myself, I say to her, there is an upwelling of alterity that can, inshallah, generate ripples of slantways thinking.

We are told we must articulate elaborate schemas, but I tell her there is something to be said for the stubborn insistence of simply being who you are, where you are. And then, from my skull, I pull out a tuft of cloud, limned and yielding, and I present it to her.

2. Half Moon Bay, Saudi Arabia, 1985

Here I am, the child on the beach.

Head craned back, her fingers dancing nonsense, she looks up and up into the blue-blue sky. Something is about to happen.

Something happens: a purling in the distance of dense shadow, a wind, sharp and sudden, that brings grit to scour her skin, to sting her eyes, to make her parents, in the distance, shout.

It is a shamal, a vast storm of sand and dust that has roared its way across three deserts to reach the eastern edge of the peninsula. It is a shamal, and in an instant gone is the sun and the horizon, gone are the shouting parents and the blue-blue sky.

Suspended in the shamal's swirl of airborne earth, the child is alone, with nothing to separate her from the sand and the sky and the raging wind.

It is my earliest memory, and I remember a strange and soaring joy.

3. Khobar, Saudi Arabia, 2016

There is boomtown energy on the pavement tonight. Densely clustered bodies crowd the curb, sand-weathered vehicles slide past, and the electric clatter of neon is always in the eye. From across the busy highway comes the salt scent of the sea and all around me the crowd heaves: there are black limes to buy for dinner, paper cups of karak chai to sip, children and errands to tend. There are men in crisp white thobes, little girls wearing salwar kameez with scattershot sequins, and two whispering boys holding hands beneath a blinking street lamp. There is a honk from a taxi behind me, a fume of squalling cats, the sizzle of lamb on a spit. A stray elbow nudges me into a shop window; I see Waterford crystal and vacuum cleaners and piles of snaking rubber tubes. And up, up, hanging from the ceiling, there is a trio of dolls with black eyes swaying. I walk on into the shifting vista of faces, into the elbows and the gleaming teeth and the soft crush of strange bodies.

It is night but the heat of the sun is still sighing off the street and the asphalt is warm through the soles of my shoes. I have sweated through my bra and my socks and even the filmy fabric of my abaya is damp and clinging to the skin at my throat. In this part of the souq they sell raw meat and fresh roses and small birds that tremble in baskets made of wicker and straw. To my right, a hawker chants about his cumin, his cardamom, his limes, his cinnamon, his saffron. He pinches something dark between his fingers and tells the crowd to smell. A man leans out of a shop – sister, do you want a scarf? I'm already wearing a scarf but mine is black and the scarf in his hands is a shocking yellow corded through with sequins, and for a moment I consider. The building on the corner is covered in flyers searching for roommates: *Pinoy wanted, Pinoy only, Pinoy required*. I walk past the mosque and the bakery and the row of electronics stores where TVs line the walls. I pass an antiques shop selling blue furniture from India and a chai shop and a coffee shop and a silversmith and a cobbler. A small boy, his hair grown out long, runs by me, and his laugh is the shriek of a bird. Here is the shambling walk of the pushcart man, here is the bowlegged splay of moonlight in the dusty clouds, and here is the heady scent of fine dates going soft in the heat. Time is pouring out of me like sweat and I'm feeling good, coming apart at the seams.

Khobar was a humble fishing village until oil, discovered in commercial quantities in 1938 at nearby Dammam oil well No. 7, changed everything. The village became a town became a city, digesting soil and distance, blooming arteries of asphalt and speed to support the infrastructure of the burgeoning oil industry. Into the new airport flowed workers from around the world, so to this day Khobar remains the only city in the Kingdom where foreigners make up a majority of the population.

7

Walking on, I repeat the words I see on the signs I pass, reveling in the bounce of their consonants, the disparate perfection of their vowels – dhahab, al tihaf, al lali, fifty-percent-off closing sale. I blink and I sniff and I sway and I blink. The glorious street is glorious in its chaos of shapes and speeds and times, the slow and the fast, the crooked and the straight, the tall and the stooped; it is all here and in being here it is glorious. A tall slice of a man emerges from a tailor shop in a thobe of blue – the shock of it. Never before a thobe like this. Amid a sea of white this thobe is the sky distilled, a rogue wave coursing the shore, an indigo so potent that people on the street stop and stare. I stop and stare. When he passes there is the scent of the sea – I think I can taste salt – and there is the urge to reach out and grab a corner of his sleeve, a flapping wave of hem, to ask *why*.

I approach an intersection, look left and right, and left and right again, and grab hold of my abaya so I can run without tripping. It is a Khobar street and there are the things of the Khobar street: the hungry cats with their soft angel paws, the honking of wayward taxis, and the night sky with its dusting of stars. The ruhh of this block, of this neighborhood, of this city, demands speed, and so I walk faster, winding myself deeper into the night. I was born here and I learned to walk on these streets, in the dim back alleys and crowded sidewalks, and I have never stopped. Now, amid the buzz of this modern city, I search out the ley lines of my youth, looking for the old streets with the stories that I remember, the old streets with the stories I still want to tell. Something inside of me, fomented in some subterranean passage, says *go* – and I do.

4.

A galvanizing failure: I tried to write a book of facts, a dispensation of needful information about the Dilmuns, the

Parthians, the Babylonians, the Jabrids, all of the people who called this land their land before those of us here now called it our land.

I wanted to chart the flow of people and tongues and cultures over the millennia, all of them passing through the Gulf, blending and folding into one another, becoming one another. I wanted to trace language and tradition through gauzy, manufactured borders, to find the truth that we have all been someone else before. I would make of the facts a battlement, a bridge, a seduction. Together we would study the ancient and realize that the scope of time erases many things, that in a thousand centuries we can see through skin and bones like windowpanes.

This book was something akin to memoir, but the more I wrote of it the more I realized that my memories were unstable, that in each visitation a new detail would rise to prominence or recede into fog, so that my past was a perpetually foreign landscape.

Hold this idea if I ever write my story

What's more, as I wrote, I realized I didn't want to exist on the page as a thing that was fixed or certain. Knowing that all memoir is fiction and that all fiction is memoir, and that what arises along the turbulent horizon in between is inherently transcultural, I wanted to make a useful performance of the past and the present, to slip around the facts to tell *a* truth.

More than anything, I wanted to keep alive the possibility of motion, the potential to veer and drift, to become a story never told before.

5.

The stories we hear about autism tend to follow a predictable trajectory. Autism is currently described in clinical literature as 'autism spectrum disorder', which is diagnosed by observation that looks for lifelong differences in socialization and communication, restricted repetitive patterns of behavior, and sensory differences. Sweeping stereotypes have persisted in popular culture since the condition was first described in 1943. These include the belief that all autistic people are the same, that autistic people do not experience empathy, have no sense of humor, are unintelligent, are incapable of insight into themselves or others, have no desire for friendship, and much more.

As M Remi Yergeau writes, throughout autism's diagnostic history theories have proliferated that reflect 'a persistent disbelief in the capacities of autistic people to be volitional, to be social, and to be selves.'[1] Yergeau observes that autistic individuals are often seen as unstoried, with autistic autobiographies characterized as 'lacking narrative structure and coherence, as lacking rhetorical facility and audience awareness, and as lacking self-reflection.' These theories and assessments, along with the stories about autism that abound in popular culture, have been used to undermine 'the very humanity' of autistic individuals.[2]

6.

New stories emerge. Other ways of knowing bloom, uprooting what was once considered irrefutable fact. In this fluctuating moment, autistic people, long excluded from contributing to the narrative surrounding autism, are telling their own stories, transforming our understanding of what autism is, how it appears, and how it is experienced.

Majia Holmer Nadesan suggests that it can be useful to view autism not merely as an embodied biological fact, but also as a state of being that emerges from within the cultural stories that we tell about what behavior is normal – and what behavior is decidedly not – and how these stories create the diagnostic category of autism and determine who falls within its bounds.[3]

Autism itself, its very meaning and its fluctuating borders, is still contentious. There is not, it seems, only one story to be told, but a myriad, and they churn and conflict, converge and ripple. [Reflecting this roiling action, Yergeau proposes that autism 'is a mode of becoming, is continuous motion that defies the clinical.'⁴

This notion appeals to me, in the way of aliens and stardust and space shuttles and shamals.]

7. Manama, Bahrain, 2017

Culture, too, is a mode of becoming.

It is noon in the alley of tea and my friend is speaking to me about ornate balconies and churning rivers and sour black limes that come from Indonesia by way of Oman. Blue sheets hang over our head, snapping in the wind, and at the end of the alley a group of boys, swathed in cigarette smoke, are watching a football match on a TV.

Whenever my friend makes a particularly good point, he brandishes his tea glass high into the air. He is now telling me that many of the souq's most celebrated architectural elements are a testament to the Gulf's transcultural past.

'Like the mashrabiya,' he says, naming a style of projecting latticework window, of which the souq boasts many finely carved specimens. 'It's from Egypt. Or maybe Iraq. And the wind towers,' he continues, referring to the tall roof structures used before air-conditioning to funnel wind into interior rooms, 'they come from Persia.'

Moving onto the topic of food, he scrutinizes Khaleeji cuisine, speaking about kabsa and shawarma, tikka and luqaimat, tracing influences that come and go between India and Lebanon, Turkey and Greece. Then he's on to Khaleeji music, charting the syncopation and drums from East Africa, the stringed instruments from India, the melodies from the

Levant. Next, he examines the folklore of the region – the ancient stories of an old woman with the legs of a donkey, and little boys who fly like falcons toward the sun – tales with furred verbs and toothy nouns. Stories, it seems, are somehow both the most rooted and the most transient artifacts of all, inflected with strange soils and beguiling hints of distant horizons.

The Gulf has been a site of intense cultural heterogeneity for millennia, with influences funneling in and influences funneling out, and my friend is eager to chart the history of this cross-pollination. But, as he talks, I am reminded of questions posed by Arianna Dagnino: 'What is authentic and what is not? What has ever been?' and 'Who/what is the Other and who/what is not?'[5]

Consider the criteria that tell us where a person is from: passport, name, place of birth, the way we pronounce the word dijjaj, the way we wrap our scarf or style our beard. Collected, they seem significant, the way signifiers are meant to. But scattered, examined, pulled at, they weaken. Taken individually, they seem almost fragile.

There was a time when I was interested in dissecting the intricacies of where and when cultural flows overlapped, merged, diverged. Like my friend, I wanted to map each intersection and chart every origin story. Now, though, I am weary of this project. Go back far enough and all you find are interstices, everywhere you look.

It is a paradox that intrigues me, that cultures are distinct expressions of a community's way of life: their singularity being worthy of regard, but also comprised of endlessly changing currents that cannot always be parsed. After all, there is not a moment of stasis we can point to that represents a culture at its purest, most fundamental form, a moment after which all changes can be considered deviations from the so-called norm. Cultures are not static ready-made frameworks but roiling, mutating processes; cultures funnel through us, as something we *do* they are not nouns but verbs.

And in their verbing action cultures slosh with tidal wave shamelessness beyond their not-so-watertight borders. And even within themselves they are varied, perceived and expressed differently from person to person. Just as there is no single moment in time when a culture can be considered pure, there is no single person within a culture who embodies it in its most authentic form, just as there is no single point on a map where one culture definitively ends and a neighboring culture definitively begins.

Ilija Trojanow and Ranjit Hoskote capture this notion by describing culture as a vast river fed by numerous forgotten tributaries, explaining that:

> [. . .] the river's official name conceals the truth of its composition; while the nametag passes into legend and lexicon, the ancestry of confluences becomes invisible [. . .] Our history, regulated by concepts of singularity and pure origin, is as much a cartographer's invention as the great river. By taking a certain tableau of it to represent culture's form and essence, it mistakes a snapshot of the river for its whole course [. . .] In the same way, the confluences of every culture are concealed, and homogenizing foundational myths are installed in their place.[6]

In this way, they contend, we remain unaware of the kaleidoscopically varied sources of our own cultures, believing them to be timelessly unchanging and unerringly pure, oblivious to the truth: 'no confluence, no culture'.[7]

8. Khobar, Saudi Arabia 2018

My friend has just gotten her driver's license and she picks me up in her father's old car. The city we pass through is in a celebratory mood – just a few days ago police officers were handing out roses at intersections to female drivers because this week women have been granted the right to drive. My friend presses down on the accelerator and the car, timeworn and stately, carries us out of the city and into the desert.

It is a season of change. Among much else, movie theaters are reopening, music concerts and art exhibitions and film festivals are happening all the time, restaurant sections that separate families and women from single male diners are becoming obsolete, and some shops are beginning to stay open during prayer time. There is even some talk that tourist visas will soon be a reality and Saudi Arabia will, for the first time, open its doors to sightseeing visitors. If I had tried to imagine all of this just a few years ago, I wouldn't have been able to. But, now that it is here, now that it is happening, it is remarkable how quickly our stories of self and place can shift.

For an hour we drive, aimless and happy. We stop for gas in the middle of nowhere and then drive in the other direction, circling the city, imagining ourselves endlessly spiraling around it, finding new approaches to take, new pathways of perception. Wind scuffs the dunes, twisting snakes of it slither across the asphalt, and in the distance, yes, there are camels. A shamal is coming and the herd is moving away from it in long loping steps, their heads like periscopes far above everything else.

When we have driven for so long that we are stiff and aching with the need to get out and move, to let our own bodies carry us through the world, my friend drives me home. A bright cord of connection is pulling yesterday toward us very quickly, and perhaps tomorrow we will feel the same as today: like everything is possible, and always has been.

9.

I have a virtual meeting with three writers who have never been to the Gulf who tell me I am writing the Gulf wrong. It is not right, they say, that I am not writing about the expected topics – topics I predict before they even say the words, because their understanding of the Gulf is rooted in stereotypes they have taken as fact; stereotypes that portray the region as insular, monolithic, unchanging. They tell me I should be writing from the inside out, they say it is imperative that my work reveals and explains. They tell me I am writing about oil-boom cities that shouldn't exist. They tell me if I don't comment on the veil I am being solipsistic.

In response, I describe to them the watery permutations of a love letter written to the Gulf from the Gulf. I tell them that a thousand years ago Hofuf was a bustling market town connected to regional trade networks, that the Gulf has been saturated with various cultural flows for millennia, that it is, in fact, a region of ancient cosmopolitanism. I explain my thoughts on the difference between writing about and writing from. I ask why the Gulf should write the stories the rest of the world expects. I use the word stereotype, I use the word reductive, I use the words al ghareeb and ruhh al makan. I say things about the potential of writing that performs the radical act of normalcy, writing that slips between tropes to reveal 'the other' as mundane.

Moving on, they tell me that the novel's narrator feels like an open window pulling in the world, they tell me they want a plot, characters, something other than the street. They call the text surreal, they call it strange, they call it disturbing. They remark on its odd sensory details and setting descriptions, they say it has an 'extraordinary implicit animism'. They want cohesion. They insist there must be linear thoroughfares running throughout the writing or else readers will turn away, lost.

I ask what is the self without place and what is place without self, and can either exist removed from the other?

They say that my writing is warped, shattered.

I say it is a crooked street that goes exactly where I want to go.

10. Muharraq, Bahrain, 2019

It is a night at the end of spring and I am at the opening of an art gallery. There are performance artists in the parking lot leaping off of ramps to twist their bodies into impossible shapes, and two men with long hair who are projecting swirling lights onto the side of the building. At this time of year, it is still conceivable we might get rain: clouds gather just off-shore and occasionally there is the low sound of thunder, like something in the distance breaking. The sound of it settles in my chest; when it thunders, I thunder.

Inside the gallery, everyone seems much younger than me, and stylish and eager and loud. There are men in leather jackets and women in elegant abayas that drag in silk puddles along the floor. Waiters move through the crowd with soft drinks on trays balanced on their hands, and cigarette smoke from outside curls in through open windows. Standing at the edge of the room, next to a series of photographs of an old man's worn, scarred hands, I tell a small circle of people about my recent meeting, in which I received the admonition that in my writing I must explain. The message is clear, I think: there are neutral spaces from which stories are allowed to spring, and from these neutral spaces (which, of course, are not at all neutral, only rendered that way) any kind of story can be told. From these neutral spaces there is no outsider that must be considered, only an unacknowledged assumption of understanding.

But if you step outside this neutral space, it is assumed that your stories will still be oriented toward it. You will still

16

write about what it expects and you will explain yourself in a way it will understand. What the individual artist wants to express is irrelevant, because when audiences from this neutral space say they want a diversity of expression what they often really want is their own opinions repeated back to them in a 'foreign' accent.

Unaware of the contextual nuances at play in the rest of the world, the gaze from this so-called neutral space is often unable to see the dimensions of meaning unfolding on canvas or in sculpture; the fluencies missed by those unaware that whole conversations are taking place without them.

It is interesting, those of us gathered at the edge of the art gallery agree, what places are allowed to be perceived as neutral and what places are expected to make a spectacle of themselves for ease of understanding. The Gulf, it seems, is always expected to perform.

A Khaleeji artist tells us a story from his time at school abroad in the US, where he was asked why the art he makes – gauzy, chaotic fabric installations – isn't explicitly about the Gulf or religion or politics, or any of the things people expect him to make art about because of where he is from.

His eyes twinkle behind rimless glasses when he tells us he insists on refusing to perform to expectations. 'Whatever you want,' he declares, 'I will not give you.'

11. Thuqbah, Saudi Arabia, 2018

A thousand sunlights sequin the street and I blink and I blink and I blink. Beneath a sunblasted sky I walk, listening to the stories that bubble up from the ferment of the asphalt, stories sticky with their own kind of memory from the vast and vaster. Geologic, tricky, I can just make out the rendering of tectonic plates beneath the scurry of traffic, the tender perching memory of long ago barasti huts on the shoreline. As I walk there is the desire to swallow the street, even as I am swallowed by the street. I find alleys I remember from childhood, dank and fogged with reek, and I know that they will exist like this forever because they exist only to me.

Wild green parrots fall like shards of glass from the sky, sharp and then sharper. I can feel the elegant tilt of this continent as I walk; if I let go, I think I could fall forever toward the sea. Toward the sea, I am walking toward the sea, to where the old dhows used to ply the green waves, loaded with teak or pearls or silver gasping fish, where half a century ago my grandmother knelt by a dead shark and decided to write about death as if it were a curious entanglement. To the sea, then, always to the sea, to the place where it meets the ever-shifting dunes.

I don't want to keep writing the city in the old, straight ways. I want to veer and make beholden a weirder inroad of knowing. The old way had its uses, it was a hand emerging from the shadows to beckon. But now, context seems like explanation which seems like justification which seems like the speech of another. In this way, context in context claims objectivity, but context in the tingling world of the real is a flight of gulls banking on thermal winds, their shriek a tumult of laughter falling from the vault of heaven. Melt now, melt now, into the city.

The story of the city and the story of the self is discordant, fragmented, disrupted; not because it is fundamentally thus, but because it is thus from certain vantage points. We alter things with our attention, changing them irrevocably. Understanding this, I know that I am an unreliable narrator, changing the life I seek to write about through the act of writing about it. The city I walk through today will not be the city that I walk through tomorrow, just as the self walking through the city today will not be the self walking through the city tomorrow. Perhaps this motion, then, is the only thread of continuity: a perpetual moving forward to see what it is that will happen next.

For me, the experience of moving through urban space feels like the clearest, most potent way to *read* a city, to know through the influx of sensory details the paths of resonance and meaning that have accrued over time. In this, walking has always been a way of finding stories that hold a different quality of light, that reveal a core of radiant significance.

There is nothing linear but, viewed through a homogenized perspective, there is something of a lineage: there have always been people who have walked like this, doggedly stalking not a person but a place. There was Walter Benjamin, writing obsessively about the Paris arcades. There was André Breton and his Surrealists, who crossed their cities guided by unconscious desires, wondering how long they might 'retain this sense of the marvelous suffusing everyday existence.'[8] Then there were the psychogeographers of the Situationist International, who, as one-time member Abdelhafid Khatib wrote, examined the impact of place on human behavior in order to potentially transform urban life.[9] Then there is mythogeography, a term coined by Phil Smith to describe a multi-layered, subjective way of experiencing place with a transformative attentiveness to the many stories that exist at a single time,[10] and Tina Richardson's schizocartography, which is a means of apprehending place as inherently unsettled and fluid, with the aim of allowing for heterogeneous interpretations that challenge dominant conceptions.[11] In order to practice these psychogeographies, these disparate stalkings of place, psychogeographers implement a practice known as *dérive* (drift), where they move quickly through urban space with no preordained plan, recording their impressions.

When I'm moving through the city on a drift, I am often swept away by wayward waves that drag me off course, which is fitting as the word *dérive* is overflowing with liquid connotations: its Old French antecedent refers to pouring and flowing, while its Latin root refers to the act of diverting a stream.[12] I've learned by now not to fight these rogue trajectories, but to simply go where they insist I go.

On a drift, everything is liquid.

12.

Autism is a liquid place with liquid borders.

As a clinical diagnosis its parameters have shifted and roiled, expanded and transformed. Even in the *Diagnostic and Statistical Manual of Mental Disorders*, the DSM – the clinical authority in the US when it comes to diagnostics – the criteria for making a diagnosis of autism spectrum disorder have changed over its various editions. The landscape of autism, then, is a place of uncertainty and equivocation.

For decades, the dominant understanding of autism was primarily based on boys who expressed their autistic characteristics in a specific range of behavior that was thought to encompass the entirety of autism.[13] It is only in recent years that experts have begun to acknowledge that the way autism can be expressed and experienced varies widely from autist to autist. There is now a growing awareness that basing diagnosis on observable behavior rather than a person's internal experience has meant generations of autistic people, especially those who are adept at masking their autistic traits, have gone undiagnosed.

Autistic girls, for example, are much less likely to be identified than autistic boys, particularly girls with high IQs.[14] Instead of autism, these autistic girls are frequently diagnosed (or incompletely diagnosed) with borderline personality disorder, obsessive compulsive disorder, or ADHD – anything, it seems, but autism. Eighty percent of autistic girls remain unidentified at the age of eighteen, which can have significant consequences in regards to their mental health.[15]

Reflecting the growing understanding that autism is not so much a set of externally observable behaviors but the inner experience of the individual, autistic people commonly describe autism as a different 'operating system' for the brain. This comparison makes clear that all aspects of an autistic person's experience are shaped by their being autistic. Autism, then, is best understood not as something overlaid atop a non-autistic person, but as something that is intrinsic to who the autistic person fundamentally is.

Autism being a spectrum does not refer to an imaginary line that runs from 'zero autism' to 'maximum autism' along which each autistic person is placed to gauge how autistic they are. All autistic people are fully autistic. Rather, the spectrum is more often likened to a color wheel, wherein each autistic trait that a person has – such as language usage, executive function, special interests, routines, sociality, attention regulation, sensory awareness, information processing, or repetitive behaviors – exists somewhere within a possible range. At a glance, it reflects the fact that no two autistic individuals are the same and will express their autistic natures in vastly different ways.

We are still not sure of the exact why of autism, but it is increasingly believed to be multifactorial, meaning it arises from a convergence of causes.[16]

In other words, as with cultures, it might be accurate to say: no confluence, no autism.

13.

While most people experience time in a linear, consecutive fashion – picture an arrow flying out of the past, slicing through the present, and heading off into the future – there are those who contend that some autistic people can experience the past, present, and future simultaneously – picture a maelstrom swirling around a single focal point. In this view, aspects of autism commonly seen as simply 'disordered' could arguably be better understood as the consequences of an individual grappling with the overwhelming experience of drifting through time.[17]

In other words, it might be accurate to say: the autistic mind is a time-traveling mind.

14.

Time is going strange and within it I am going stranger.

I remember Krakow sweet syrup and mangosteen lopped into sour yogurt; I remember all the dry Octobers when perilous summer heat finally relented and the sky bloomed blue again; I remember Ramadan when the streets went thick with Vimto deliveries, boxes of purple cordial glowing rhapsodies in the sun, and the way they sometimes burst, bottles shattering under the weight of it all, running into the gutter where we would play in the mess, fingers stained and crawling with ants; I remember the titans of the skywalk dropping marbles on the crowd below, marbles of green-spitting-gold and yellow-bleeding-blue falling from the sky for us to carry home in pockets, treasured; I remember the night a man nobody knew tumbled from the overpass and died, and the way the women keened at the cold store with grief for this man who had no family and no friends, no children and no wife, this sad all-alone night-falling man who maybe jumped into traffic wanting this world no more; I remember alley cats and alley rats and stray dogs loping through alleys where there was no friend to find; I remember every prayer call I have ever heard; I remember goat roasts in the star-spackled black forever night of the desert; I remember Iftars with the streets taken up by the longest rugs and plastic sheets for tables, the steaming chicken and gleaming rice; I remember Green Jack standing on the corner telling the crowd that if we only had the vision for it we would know there are no villains, that saints and sanctities were all around

22

us; I remember leaves falling in bright February, oceans of yellow, leaves tumbling in the wind, and leaves in the gutter, and leaves leaving traces of somber spring; I remember black taxis and red sunsets, red buses and blue dawns; I remember it all and I remember it now and, in this remembering, I wonder if these remembrances, with their singed fingertips and marble treasures and missing teeth, with their sticky bottles and sour yogurts and weeping yellow February trees, ever remember me.

15. Hofuf, Saudi Arabia 1992

The dark interior of the cave smells like the rubbery insides of my Gulf War gas mask: stale, sweet, musty. The scent beckons, it pulls me in deeper.

I lose the sound of the others who are still outside, draping the ground with picnic blankets and unpacking sandwiches. Holding a hand to the wall of the cave's interior, I begin my circumnavigation of the space. The wall feels like velvet, like smoke, like the pelt of a gentle animal. Alone and pensive, I glide alongside it, wrestling with a new understanding that has recently been made clear to me.

I am ten years old and beginning to understand what it means for there to be a mismatch between where I am from and where I am *from*. Being a Saudi-born American, from a family that has lived in the Kingdom for three generations but is not *from* here, is not strange to me but I am beginning to realize that it is certainly strange to others. I am starting to understand why, when people ask if I am American, the answer I want to give is 'yes and . . .'

At home, before this dawning comprehension, I hadn't known to separate in my mind the music we listened to, with Umm Kulthum on one side and George Strait on another. I didn't know that Easter and Eid were so very different. To me, the best dip for French fries was hummus, and tacos for lunch and kabsa for dinner was unremarkable, as was the constantly burning oud, organizing our shopping trips around prayer time, watching Captain Majed followed by Mister Rogers, and our Arabic-infused English, where each language was simply another way for words to dance. I knew to kiss ladies on both cheeks when I made their acquaintance, to say alhamdulillah when someone asked me how I was and mashallah when I gave a compliment. The rhythms and touchstones of everyday life in Saudi Arabia were simply the fundamental fabric of the way the world worked. I could not imagine anything else. Saudi did not seem like an unusual place for me to live because it was simply the only home I had ever known.

I don't yet know the word 'interstice' or the meaning of 'transcultural', but I do know the word 'foreigner', and I know that in the Gulf, because of the citizenship requirements, most foreigners are usually foreigners forever. One day my family and I will have to leave, and with no tourist visas; when that day comes, I know it will mean leaving forever. I have walked with friends as they said goodbye to everything they knew. Their families had exit-only visas and one-way tickets out, their fathers retiring or transferring or just leaving to find home somewhere else. And so, I have walked with these friends through the parks, down the streets, around our houses, by the school, knowing they would never return, would never see this place again, no matter how much they might want it. They would take pictures, press bougainvillea petals into the pages of scrapbooks, and pour sand in runny handfuls into glass bottles with cork stoppers. Doing this alongside them taught me that home was a place I would one day be required to leave, and it gave me a sort of double vision: I could see what was in front of me as it was, but I also began seeing it as the memory of a place I would eventually never be able to see again.

I move to the middle of the cave, kicking up clouds of dust with every step I take, and I twirl around, feeling like a dust mote spin-spinning in the dark.

Then I stop.

I stand very still in the center of the cave. I let my eyes adjust to the absence of light, and then I linger there, in the stubborn darkness, adjusting my breath so that eventually it is only another silence in the silence.

16. Riyadh, Saudi Arabia, 1994

Stuck to my lip stuck to my lip stuck to my lip, the hem of my headscarf is stuck to my lip. The hem of my headscarf is stuck to my lip and it keeps being stuck to my lip. I am plucking it off and this motion, this tender yank, is all I feel I have done for hours. New bought for Riyadh, the headscarf is gauzy and delicate and clings stubbornly to my de rigueur Body Shop kiwi lip-glossed lips and I worry all this yanking will undo it, that out here in public in front of everyone I will come undone.

My sixth-grade class has just landed at the Riyadh airport and the place is full of glaring fluorescent lights, miles of pale marble, and flight announcements that go booming through the air like staticky thunder. Our teacher begins the process of herding us toward a bus and, as we move off, I can hear the 4 Non Blondes blaring from one classmate's Walkman and Amr Diab from another. My classmates and I are a distillation of everything early nineties: the straps of our backpacks are doodled with Wite-Out peace signs, there are sunflowers on headscarves, and the boldest among us are wearing Doc Martens on our feet.

Our bus hurtles down the highway of a city that is towering and modern and fast. Its architecture makes everything feel important, stolid and imposing, and different from the cities I know back home in the east. We have been learning about Riyadh in school and I know that, located in the Najd, the central plain of the country, Riyadh was made the capital of the Second Saudi State in 1824 by Turki bin Abdullah Al Saud, who moved his court from Ad Dariyyah. At the time, Riyadh was one of a scattering of towns spread throughout Wadi Hanifa, but after becoming the capital it was transformed. By the turn of the century, Riyadh was enclosed by a mud-and-brick wall, guarded by towers and manned gates, but by the 1930s, the city overflowed beyond the area bounded by the wall, spreading into the surrounding date groves. The advent of cars, electricity, and a modern sewage system pushed the city limits even farther. When, in the 1950s, King Saud modernized Riyadh and relocated government institutions to the city from Mecca and Jeddah, the city's rapid expansion was truly under way.[18]

By the time of my class trip the city's proportions are staggering. Looking out the window of our speeding bus, I'm in awe of the architecture: there are towering buildings with whimsical designs, each one trying to outdo the other in stature and shock value. Taking it in, I'm talking a mile a minute to the girl sitting next to me, reciting the facts we have learned about the city in class and pointing out everything we pass that catches my attention – look at that building, look at that street, look at that car, that tree, that park, that billboard, that fountain. Words rattle out of my mouth so quickly that I trip up, my tongue and teeth unable to keep up with the bombardment of my thoughts.

I've always been told I talk too much. Words bloom and blossom and bustle their way out of me in endless shimmering streams, and, even though I get in trouble for it all the time, I never stop. I chant phrases I have heard that stick in my head and invent words and nicknames for everything; language is a wild playground where I feel like I can make magic happen. But there is another reason why I talk so much – speech is a way to shield myself from the too-muchness of the world. It always feels like the world is coming at me, too loud, too quick, too bright, too much, and, rather than squeeze shut my eyes

26

and put my hands over my ears, I use my own talking like a shield. My constant talking annoys teachers, classmates, and pretty much any adult I come into contact with – including my pre-school ballet teacher who decided my ceaseless chatter was so distracting that I was unceremoniously booted from class and told never to return.

But this constant talking is just one of the many things about me that are seen by others as odd. I have always been sort of a weird kid. I talked early, walked late, and had seizures when I spiked a fever. I take things literally, don't often realize when other people are using sarcasm, and spend most of my time so deeply absorbed in books that I live more inside their pages than I do in the real world. Hyperlexic, I taught myself to read around three years old and was flying through chapter books not long after. Fantasy and science fiction have always been my cherished favorites, but I read anything: fiction and non-fiction, highbrow and low, even the dictionary when the mood strikes. As long as it is a book, I am keen. I don't just read, though, I study what I read with intensity, taking notes and lecturing my classmates on the finer points, like J Robert Oppenheimer's role as the architect of the atomic bomb, or why a good grounding in dressage is a fundamental pre-requisite to show-jumping success. It doesn't really occur to me that other people aren't interested in the information I am sharing, because at this time in my life I mostly think of other people as an audience for whom I can perform.

I had also been put through a series of tests upon entering a new school and was told afterwards that I was 'gifted'. This is a term that, by twelve, I am having an increasingly complicated relationship with; what started out to be an apparently positive thing has mostly turned out to be a burden, as adults use the knowledge of how I scored on those tests to judge me and find me lacking. I now most often hear the terms 'gifted' and 'genius' coupled with the admonition that I am lazy, obstinate, and failing to live up to expectations.

There are other idiosyncrasies, like my bossy overbearing nature, my analytical way of thinking and my need to categorize and compare everything, my rigid adherence to routine, and my overpowering emotions. And then there are my tics. I sniff and blink repetitively, which gets me made fun of by classmates and adults alike. The resulting humiliation only exacerbates my stress, which in turn makes the tics worse. Then there are the quirks that get me accused of being a fussy drama queen, like my avoidance of silverware, which makes my teeth crackle like they are electrified, or my hatred of ticking clocks, which has me beg my obliging grandmother to trawl her house for any offending timepiece and hide it away in a drawer for the entire duration of my visit, or the circuitous route I take whenever I am at the grocery store so I can avoid the suffocating stench of the detergent aisle. I am often told by adults to calm down, to get a grip, to stop being so weird and annoying, but this only confuses and upsets me because I don't know any other way to be.

From today's vantage point it is clear that all of this could be an indicator of autism. Perhaps not the factors taken individually, but considered all together, and, to the extent that they impacted my ability to function 'normally', they were good pointers that an autism assessment would have been a reasonable idea. But during my childhood no one considered such a thing. At that time, most experts believed that girls were rarely autistic, and, if they were, they typically did not use spoken communication and would also have an intellectual disability. There was not yet a general understanding that autism could present in a wide variety of ways, or that many autistics were adept at hiding their struggles and mimicking neurotypical behavior.

It is also common for some autistic people to get through childhood relatively OK until puberty hits and the hormonal storm – as well as increasingly complex social pressures and intensifying expectations and responsibilities – pushes them past their ability to cope. Puberty is often a time when comorbid conditions associated with autism (or conditions associated with the struggle of being autistic with no diagnosis, self-knowledge, or accommodations) can emerge, such as anxiety, depression, complex post-traumatic stress disorder, and obsessive-compulsive disorder.

When I turned eleven, the racing, leaping thoughts that had always characterized my mental processes, and the ruminative, heated intensity with which they operated, ratcheted up to another level. I didn't know what was happening, all I knew was that seemingly overnight my brain had become a vicious, implacable beast. I was battered by frightening intrusive thoughts that made me think I was always on the brink of death, or that someone in my family was about to die. I felt the need to perform mental compulsions, cogitating endlessly on these terrifying thoughts in an effort to neutralize them. Even metaphysical quandaries were enough to keep me locked inside my mind in spirals of ever-increasing panic as I could not figure out, for example, if human actions were governed by free will or by fate. OCD is a condition that leaves a person fixated upon and terrorized by doubt and ambiguity, so when the brain finds a question that can't be solved, like philosophical conundrums that have occupied the greatest minds in history, rather than it being a diverting thought exercise, finding the solution feels like a matter of life and death.

So relatable!

At night, when I was supposed to be asleep, I would stay awake rearranging items in my room – the chair in the corner of my bedroom needed to be angled just right, the blanket at the foot of my bed had to hang just so, the reading lamp on the table had to be at a specific spot, and the closet door needed to be propped open the exact perfect amount. This was not about tidiness – my room was as messy as ever – it had to do with the way objects were positioned in orientation to each other. In my mind there was an underlying field of rightness beneath the thin scrim of reality that, while I could not see it, could certainly be felt – felt with an intensity akin to fire ants swarming up my legs. If I tried to ignore my brain's shrill demands, to tell myself that this was objectively pointless, the panicky, doomed wrongness of these compulsions not being properly completed would glow hotter and hotter until it was the only thing I could think about. The demands were so ruthless and so relentless that it felt easier to just give in rather than white-knuckle it through the agony of resisting.

All of this behavior was suggestive of OCD, but at the time I doubt I even knew what OCD was. And, if I did, I'm sure my knowledge only extended to the popular image of the condition, that of washing your hands excessively. But many people with OCD aren't concerned about cleanliness or hand washing, which makes the prevalence of that stereotype especially pernicious. The co-occurrence of OCD and autism is significant. Autistic people are two times as likely to be diagnosed with OCD as non-autistic people, and people with OCD are four times as likely to be autistic as people without OCD.[19] One study even found that forty-seven percent of OCD patients surveyed had clinically significant autistic traits.[20]

As a child, I didn't know any of this. And I didn't tell anyone what was happening. So, as I moved through adolescence and into my teenage years, I struggled with this in silence, taking it as confirmation that all the things people had ever said about me being a freak were true.

Throughout the whole of that day in Riyadh I talk, not caring who I am talking to, not caring if they are listening, or if what I am saying is particularly interesting to them. We visit a museum, the Diplomatic Quarter, and Murabba Palace, but it isn't until our bus pulls up next to Masmak Fort, and I see its tawny flanks rising up into the sky, that I am finally struck silent.

The fort is different from anything we've seen in Riyadh. It feels resolutely old, and not polished for visitors. It looks precisely like what it is: a fortress built for strength. There is something in its formidable features that makes it more impressive than the tallest of the city's skyscrapers. Built between 1865 and 1895, from unbaked bricks and mud plaster, the fort has an immense watchtower at each corner. Inside are storerooms, a mosque, diwaniyeh, treasury, and barracks, all grouped around colonnaded courtyards.

My class files off the bus and moves toward it and, if our teacher is talking, I am not listening. Mouth hanging open, no words coming out, I silently approach the citadel in wonder. I have heard stories of Masmak all my life. Considered the birthplace of the modern Saudi nation, it was here in 1902 that King Abdulaziz Al Saud led his daring pre-dawn raid to recapture Riyadh. On that January night, King Abdulaziz and his band of men scaled the city walls and crept their way through the darkness toward the fort where they would confront – and defeat – their opponents. This night is the stuff of legend, a nucleus around which the story of the nation has been forged. After the victory at Masmak, King Abdulaziz would go on to unify the central Arabian Peninsula under his rule as the Kingdom of Saudi Arabia.

To my eyes, Masmak appears to rise seamlessly from the bedrock of the desert below, as if it is hewn from the earth itself. I drift toward the fort's huge wooden door. There is a small opening in the center, called an al-khokha, a defensive feature that allows only one person to pass through at a time without the full door having to be opened. I approach tentatively, looking for what I have heard is still there – and there it is. Embedded deep into the wood is a gnarled spearhead. During the scramble of hand-to-hand combat in 1902, the King's cousin, Abdullah bin Jalawi, flung his spear with such force that it lodged inches deep into the thick wood.

I reach up and poke at it, trying to gain purchase, trying to discern the precise point where the hard steel ends and the splintery wood begins, but beneath the scrabble of my fingers it all feels the same.

17. Dhahran, Saudi Arabia, 2000

Dust and sand and smoke in my mouth, campfire blazing like an Earth-bound star. All around me jebels clutch at the night with skeletal fingers.

'Someone change the music!'

Guitar and drums and drums and drums, we dance until we can't stop laughing and then we fall to the ground next to the fire and ask someone, anyone, for a light.

We watch headlights down below emerging from a neighborhood of frangipani-lined streets and cookie-cutter houses that have neat, American-style front lawns and basketball hoops in their driveways. We watch the bigness of the night pull up sparks from the fire. We watch one another, faces flickering and eyes shining and teeth gleaming in the dark. Most of us grew up here, some of us were born here, and soon we will all be leaving. High school graduation is weeks away and after we will leave for university.

I look around, blinking in the smoke, and try to find due north. When I think I've got it, I point to the spot, a low point between two jebels lit by the grin of the up-above moon, and I tell no one in particular that my father was a child in a little town in that direction. Then I find what I think is south, a spot beyond a fur of trees in the distance, glowing orange with construction lights, and I tell no one in particular that my mother was a child in an even littler town in that direction. No one listens. The music is too loud, my voice too low, and my words don't matter anyway because the fact that Saudi is my home three generations deep is irrelevant. I'm still leaving soon, just like foreigners almost always do.

After graduation the destinations of those of us here tonight span the globe, and the matches between nationality and destination are unpredictable. There are Saudis heading to the States, heading to London, and staying put. There is an Egyptian heading for America, Americans heading for Cairo, a Nigerian heading for Germany, a German heading for Scotland, and an American heading for London.

For the foreigners among us, this leaving will be a heavy thing, something with so much weight that even now, before it has even happened, it drags at the body. I can already feel its sludgy tides pulling at me. We know that once we graduate and leave we will likely never again return to Saudi to live. We will only come back for brief visits to see our family until our fathers retire and it is time to say goodbye forever. We know these remaining weeks could be one of the last times we will live in a place where we are understood and where we understand, where we don't have to explain to anyone that although we are not Saudi by nationality, Saudi is our home.

Most of us here tonight have had a few years longer living in Saudi than our peers. Most of our expatriate classmates moved away to go to school abroad years ago, after ninth grade, when school typically ends for expat kids and they must leave for boarding school. My mother attended boarding schools in Greece and England and my father went to boarding school in Lebanon. It was routine, the normal thing that everyone did, and there were few alternatives. Childhood felt like a funnel in which we were always being prepared for the moment of our departure, and the nearer we got to the end of our time here, the faster time seemed to go. I did not want to leave, but, like everyone else, after ninth grade graduation, I left.

For the first few months at my all-girls school in New England, I did nothing but cry. On the phone to family, to the girls in my dorm, to teachers, to anyone who would listen. I was disoriented and overwhelmed by a grief so sharp, so relentless, that it felt like an actual physical injury. That the school was perfectly nice only made me feel worse – what kind of person could feel this miserable at a school so many people would love to attend? I spent much of my time in the school therapist's office, shredding tear-soggy tissues and trying to explain the enormity of what it was I was feeling. She listened

33

patiently, but what I couldn't explain, not even to myself, was that this move had completely exceeded my ability to cope.

Autistic people can struggle with change. This is often attributed to the fact that we are believed to take in huge amounts of input from the surrounding world, something that can make even everyday life overwhelming. This is why structure and routine can feel blissful, they serve as containers in which we can thrive, sanctuaries in which we are free to experience the intensity of our existence in a way that we can predictably regulate. But when that predictability is overnight replaced with the complete change of everything you have ever known – like being fifteen years old, 6,000 miles away from home, living in a completely foreign place in the raucous setting of a dorm – mental circuitry gets fried. Those first months at boarding school, mine was a smoldering wreck. The inside of my head felt like it was living through a non-stop emergency, like trying to sleep, eat, socialize, study, relax, all while fire alarms are blasting and you think you smell smoke.

As the months passed, while I still yearned desperately to be back home in the Gulf, I began to adjust. I was increasingly able to confine my crying jags to my dorm room and I took part in school plays and debate competitions, went to dances at nearby all-boys schools, and looked forward to Sunday mornings when the cafeteria filled with the smell of sizzling bacon and chocolate-chip pancakes. I made friends, albeit haphazardly, but I liked them well enough. Though, I spent as much time as I ever did escaping to my favorite refuge, eventually reading so many books from the school library that the librarian, a tiny old man usually accompanied by his two, ghostly silent Irish wolfhounds, asked me when I ever had time for anything else.

Isolated on our seemingly perpetually wintry campus, in many ways America felt as far away as ever. Most of my friends were international students who were just as new to the country as I was. We stuck together and made our own

34

rituals, like lying in bed on Saturdays doing homework and listening to Fleetwood Mac, or walking into town through slushy snowdrifts to buy candy – when I wasn't grounded to campus, that is.

Getting 'campused' was something that happened to me with drumbeat regularity because I was incapable of keeping my room clean. My room was, in fact, such a blazing example of chaos that my dorm mother would frequently pause at my open door and sneer before doling out yet another punishment. Water bottles, candy wrappers, shoes, books, and empty potato chip bags littered the floor, my desk was hidden beneath the trailing vines of a half-dead plant and towering piles of books and notebooks, and my bed was obscured beneath a pile of laundry destined to languish unfolded forever.

Laundry was its own particular problem. I could never remember to do it. And on the rare occasions that I did remember, the steps required to collect it from where it was scattered around my room and put it into my hamper to carry across campus to the scary, clanking machines in the damp basement were so overwhelming that I usually gave up before ever getting started. On the even rarer occasions that I did make it to the laundry room, I felt cowed by the strong smells and loud noises and could never seem to get the machines to work properly, so that my clothes were either still wringing wet when they were supposed to be dry or left claggy with the residue of laundry soap.

While at boarding school, I am beginning to become aware of the many ways I don't quite keep pace with my peers. Cutting through the positive messages I receive, the kindness and encouragement from my favorite teachers, are these failures and missteps that don't seem to make any sense. I don't know why my friends laughingly call me 'bizarre', or why people always find me too much or too weird or just plain annoying. I know that everyone is different, that most teenagers feel at times alienated and like no one understands them, and I know that everyone has their strengths and their weaknesses, but from what I can tell the girls around me aren't struggling with the things I am struggling with. But I know that more than anything I am lucky to have the life I have been given, the opportunities I have, and so I tell myself that focusing on these negatives is tantamount to being ungrateful. What I do, instead, is keep going as best I can, pretending all the while like none of it bothers me at all.

I have a picture of my dorm room from the end of that year in its typical feral state. I remember laughing as I snapped the shot, like I didn't care in the least that my filthy room was the stuff of campus legend. But what I think now, as an adult, when I look at the picture of my messy room is why didn't any of the adults punishing me stop to ask themselves if I enjoyed misplacing my possessions, forgetting assignments, or living in a state of chaos? Adults never seemed to understand how I could have been reading at a college level since elementary school while not being able to remember to get a permission slip signed, return a library book, or figure out how to work the laundry machines. No one considered that there could be a reason for this disparity between my apparent academic skill and my lack of so-called common sense, so it was always chalked up to being lazy and I was grounded, shouted at, called stupid, and worse.

I was not being lazy, though: it was an issue with executive function. Autistic people often struggle with executive function – the cognitive processes connected to our ability to do things like plan, organize, follow a schedule, regulate attention, and memory. These struggles can be exacerbated during times of change and stress, and can be further compounded if the autistic individual has ADHD – which is not unlikely as more than half of autistic individuals have traits of ADHD, and one in four children with ADHD have autistic characteristics.[21] The two have so many similarities, and are seemingly so intertwined, there have, in fact, been investigations into whether they actually may be different expressions of the same underlying phenomenon.[22]

These issues with keeping my room clean during my childhood are often seen by others at the time as moral failings on my part. They are seen as things I should be able to fix if I just work at it hard enough, and if I choose not to do that then it is evidence of laziness or obstinacy. But neurodivergence is not a lack of effort and it is not a moral failing; it is a neurological difference in perception and behavior that diverges from what society deems normal, and there are aspects of it that cannot simply be changed through sheer willpower. What forever confuses and angers me is that I am harangued and punished for my so-called lack of common sense, but my peers who do their laundry and clean their rooms are never harangued or punished for not doing the things I can do, like read half a dozen books a week. Why, I always wonder, are the things I am good at considered bonus features – unnecessary, but nice – while the things I am bad at are considered signs of inherent moral failure?

Having significant disparities between various cognitive domains, such as attention, working memory, social cognition, verbal acuity, numerical aptitude, perceptual reasoning, or analytical intelligence, is known as having a spiky cognitive profile. Spiky because, if the strengths and weaknesses are displayed visually, they form an Alpine landscape of high highs and low lows. Most people generally have relatively uniform cognitive profiles, whereas extreme disparities between cognitive strengths and weaknesses among neurodivergent individuals is so common that it is recognized as a quintessential aspect of the neurodivergent mind. Decades after leaving boarding school, after extensive cognitive testing, a neuropsychologist will tell me that aspects of my cognitive profile are so spiky, with such extreme gaps between the highs and the lows, that it is a discrepancy seen in only one percent of the population.

'Hurry up!' someone shouts.

'I am hurrying!' shouts back a boy who is rummaging through his car. He crawls out of the back seat and opens the trunk, which is filled with camping gear and a set of dented golf clubs.

A minute later he emerges triumphantly clutching a battered shisha pipe. Within minutes a blazing coal is placed carefully atop the punctured tinfoil covering the bowl and then the smell of strawberry tobacco sugars the wind.

Conversation has drifted to the topic of where we should go next. The wind is picking up, dust is getting into eyes, and everyone is restless, keen to move on, to see where else there is to be and if maybe it's better than here. I don't care where we go, I just don't want this night to end. When an argument breaks out about whose house we should go to, I get up and start to climb up the side of the jebel.

Footsteps knocking free loose pebbles, I listen as they slither in snakelike streams to the ground below. The sound is sharp, atonal; it sends a shiver up my spine. I've been climbing these jebels all my life, so even in the dark I move quickly, hesitating only when I think I see the scuttling luminous body of a camel spider, but it's only a plastic bag snared on a bush. At the top of the jebel the sound of the music coming from the parked car down below is fragile; if I turn into the wind I can make it disappear altogether.

After one year at boarding school in New England, to my relief and gratitude, my parents agreed to let me return to live in Saudi and attend high school in Bahrain. For the past two years, I have left the house at 6am, commuting across the causeway through passport control and customs, spent the day at school, then turned around to do it all over again every evening on the return journey. Coming back to live in Saudi when I was supposed to be overseas in boarding school was generally seen by others as a failure, as something reserved for wayward kids who simply couldn't cut it in their proper place.

But in my desperation to be back in the Gulf, back in a world that was familiar, that didn't matter to me. I just wanted more time here before I had to leave for good. And when I had come back, two years ago, I had thought I had a luxury of time before I had to leave again, but now it seems that those two years have vanished in an instant. Now it is time to leave all over again. Inhaling, I try to memorize the dusty scent of atomized earth that lingers atop the jebel, the subtle sweetness of the nearby thorn bushes and their tiny white flowers that tremble like moths. There are a lifetime of things I want to be sure I remember so deeply they can never be forgotten.

The last two years in Bahrain, I liked my school and I liked my friends and I liked that I was one of only a handful of American kids in my grade. But, most of all, I loved being home. I loved waking up in the morning to the ferocious blaze of the sun, to the smell of jasmine and frangipani, to hearing Arabic and kissing people on both cheeks and knowing how to move and be and speak around others once again – no longer feeling hopelessly overwhelmed and out of my depth.

But, after a lifetime of being told that I was annoying, uptight, lazy, and just *too much*, a part of me felt numb. If that was what trying my hardest had gotten me, then I decided I wouldn't try anymore. From then on, anything that I didn't understand or that I wasn't good at simply didn't matter all that much. I made friends and went to parties, but I could never shake the suspicion that I was more tolerated than liked, always lingering on the outskirts of friend groups, tenuously linked to everyone else by a single friendship. People still called me 'weird' for reasons I didn't understand. Sometimes I pretended like I wanted to be outrageous, like being seen that way was something I was intentionally cultivating, but I'm not really sure it was. I had always socialized by carrying a picture in my mind, based on movies I had watched or books I had read, which I believed were good indicators of how things would unfold if I performed a certain way. But what I couldn't

39

figure out was why things never went quite how I imagined they would. I didn't understand why few people seemed to warm up to me and why seemingly close friends dropped me without explanation. I coped with this by not thinking about it and by telling myself that it didn't really matter anyway. To make things even worse, eruptions of panic were increasingly breaking through my irreverent façade. When these bouts came on, my body told me to run, to flee, to escape, which didn't make sense because I was usually at a party or out with my friends, places where I told myself I was definitely, for sure, no doubt having so much fun.

From down below a torn piece of conversation floats up to reach me, a laughing shriek just loud enough to travel. This late at night, this high up in the jebels, time feels elastic. In school we learned that these jebels, part of the Rus Formation, are something like sixty-three million years old. My time-drifting mind tries to peer across this chronological expanse, imagining the shifting and lifting of continents, the sloshing influx of seas, the relentless grinding of the wind.

In Saudi folklore the land itself has been known to yield to the power of human emotion, as in the well-known story of Aja and Salma from pre-Islamic Arabia. Aja and Salma were teenagers who fell hopelessly in love. There are different variations of this story across the country, each region and tribe putting their own flavor into the telling, a different spin on the details. Some say that Aja and Salma were unable to be together because of Salma's controlling brothers who saw Aja as an unsuitable match, forcing the love-struck couple to run away. Others say that Aja and Salma had to run away because they were from separate tribes, tribes bristling with a long history of enmity and unwilling to allow any union to link them. Whatever the reason for their love's impossibility, in all of the Aja and Salma stories, the end is blood-soaked. After the two runaways are caught, Salma's disapproving family takes her to the top of a mountain and Aja's disapproving family takes him to the top of another mountain, and there, on those lonely, windswept peaks, painfully far apart, the two are killed.

But the story does not end here. Linger on the mountain tops where innocent blood has just been spilled, linger as the families drift away, linger as day becomes night becomes day once again, linger until the last traces of spilled blood have been taken in by the earth, linger and see what happens.

What happens is this: the two mountains, miles apart, are emboldened. Pushing their basalt and granite feet through the soil, they grind closer and closer together. According to the tales, the two mountains – one named Salma and one named Aja, part of the Shammar mountain range in the Ha'il province – came together, moved by love.

I look around, studying the pale grammar of my native land. The jebels' rising crags and steep flanks are white as bone in the moonlight. They are no mountains, but to me they have always seemed receptive, as if they are listening in their own deep way. This place has been one of the central relationships – if not *the* central relationship – in my life. As people have come and gone, these jebels have been here. This is where I came as a little girl, sharing my secrets with the hot wind, running from wild dogs, and watching golden foxes slink after quick-scuttling lizards. This desert is what I think of when I say that Saudi is home. These last weeks, everyone has been talking about how much they will miss everyone else; I know I've said as much. But I know that what I will really miss is this place.

18. London, England, 2001

The wind coming off the Thames is a living thing, cold and sharp and clawing. Squinting my eyes against the chill, I make my way toward Richmond Hill, dodging gaggles of schoolchildren and mummies pushing strollers. Lining the streets there are bakeries and cafes and posh family homes with shiny cars parked out front and the remnants of Christmas decorations still twinkling in windows. I pass a Victorian terrace house with a velvet of moss gliding up its face and a churchyard where the roots of an old oak rise up from the ground like once-buried bodies. It rained earlier and the smell of damp stone and damp earth surrounds me in a dense vegetal cloud, greening each breath I take and furring the exhale with the memory of soil.

I count pavement cracks as I walk, and then I count the curbs I must step up, and then I count the curbs I must step down, and then I count the cars that are blue, and then the cars that are green, and then the cars that are black, until I run out of things to count and I keep walking into a morning that is as cold and sharp as a ringing bell and I feel myself beginning to go slantways in my mind.

I walk faster. I breathe faster. I start looking for other slipstreams of meaning to traverse beyond the purely topographical. In quick succession, I pass a building with a plaque and a memorial fountain with a plaque and a bench with a plaque, all bearing dates at least a hundred years in the past. The past then, into the past, letting it swarm its way into my head, the marching feet, the battle drums, the tongues and the plagues, and the flames. In London – which used to be Londinium, and Plowonida, and Kaer Llundain, where there were inrushing tides of Romans, Saxons, Vikings, and Normans, whose very founding is traced to Brutus of Troy, a legendary interloper from across the sea – the past is an easy slipstream to find. London keeps its other days tightly pinned to the present; everywhere there are flashes of earlier times, earlier lives, earlier stories, that penetrate the existing moment. I've been visiting London all my life, but the riddle of its streets and damp alleys, the bewitching tangle of its old Roman roads and twelve hidden rivers, still holds the mysterious promise of something worthy of pursuit, something chronologically dislocated that could be found even here, even now, if I could just move fast enough.

Arthur Machen wrote of a London interpenetrated by other realities, a city brimming with the potential of fragmentation. In his 1935 'N', a man who has heard tales of an impossibly Edenic garden in a mundane London neighborhood visits the neighborhood in question searching for a sight of the paradise. Once there, he is told that an asylum used to operate in the area, from which a patient once escaped. The patient attempted to slip back into everyday life by renting rooms nearby. When one day the escapee exclaimed to his new landlady about the extraordinary view of an idyllic garden he could see from his room's window, a garden she knew didn't exist, the game was up and the patient was caught. 'N' does not end there, however. While the narrator has proof that the tales he has heard of a paradisical garden where a garden plainly isn't could be attributed to delusion, instead of dismissing these tales he proclaims his openness to the possibility that reality can have many streams, each shining passage coiling around the others, intermingling, breaking through.[23]

As I walk and breathe and slip through time, thinking of London's pasts, of Machen's elysian visions, of still-wild rivers secreted beneath a falsity of asphalt, there is a moment when the city and my thoughts about the city skitter: real to unreal, ordinary to malevolent, routine to horrifying. It is a quick-flash break in my deliberately seamless stream of consciousness, a blink-and-you-miss-it shudder, but I don't blink and I don't miss it and when the city wobbles between that-which-is and that-which-might-be, I know exactly what is coming.

I walk even faster, leaning into the wind, leaning into the incline of Richmond Hill, leaning my way to the very top. Down the street in one direction is the pub where I bartend, down the street in another direction is the hotel where I waitress, and up the street and around the corner is the university where I occasionally go to class. At the hotel, I circulate through wedding crowds carrying canapés and mop the floors afterward, but do so with a lurking incompetence. As a bartender I can't run the till without setting off a flurry of bleeping errors, fill drinks without them sloshing over, or keep tabs in any semblance of order. I'm so bad I'm only allowed to work the afternoon shift, when the pub is quiet, and even then I get overwhelmed and confused, which makes me smile even bigger and laugh even louder to distract from my ineptitude. Even still, I suspect it is only a matter of time before I'm fired.

When I reach the top of Richmond Hill I find it full of people, people walking their dogs, people walking themselves, and people drinking coffee from takeaway cups. I take a shaky breath and find a spot at the wrought-iron railing and lean over it, trying to catch my breath, trying to slow the frenzied rhythm of my heart. Looking down toward the meander of the Thames, I find the water silver and slow-moving. I count the boats that pass and the boats that are moored. I count bicyclists and dog walkers. I count two elderly women sharing a bench and a pastry. I count three shivering, sweatered lurchers on leashes. I count four toddlers shepherded by one harried woman. I count the beat of my heart and find that it has not slowed at all.

And, just like I knew it would, just like it always has since the start of the year, *theterrorthepanicthefearthehorrorthedread* crashes over me. In an instant my heart is too large for my ribcage and it flails like a panicked bird, knocking things loose that shouldn't be loose. In an instant my head is full of static, my head is ballooning, my head is vanishing over the horizon. In an instant there isn't enough air, there has never been enough air, there will never be enough air, so I gasp and I gasp and I gasp.

Panic attacks. That was the term the school therapist used when I told her what was happening. But those words are insubstantial, tiny nothings, four syllables of emptiness. It's like using the word 'rock' to describe Chicxulub, the six-mile-wide asteroid that slammed into the Earth and wiped out the dinosaurs. Calling it panic or anxiety makes it seem small and manageable, a vagueness that could never pose any real harm, which makes no sense because whatever this is has demolished the world that I once knew. Whatever this is has demolished the me that I once knew.

I cannot eat because I have no appetite, and when I can tolerate a few bites of food it is only a few minutes before I rush to the toilet and am sick, my body too struck with terror to keep anything down. My heart races throughout my waking hours and I cannot study because I have no ability to focus. I am increasingly unable to sit through class, sometimes lasting only a few minutes until the squelching sound of someone chewing gum, the birdlike scratching of pen on paper, or the ear-splitting thunder of my own thoughts sends me bolting from the room. Even going to class in the first place has become a near impossibility. My academic advisor tells me that my grades are in danger, that I need to get my act together and live up to my potential, but all I can do is nod silently at him, knowing nothing will change. All I want to do is hide myself away from the world and its constant onslaught of intensity, this shockwave of fear that always finds me.

What the school therapist didn't have words for, though, was the way my mind worked. Had always worked. Nothing about that had changed, what had changed was my ability to cope with it.

The thoughts, I told her, they never stop. There has never been a moment in my life when there weren't a thousand of them grabbing at me, like a swarm of small children all snatching at my arm trying to get my attention. If I, for example, thought of a car, my mind filled with a Rolodex of cars – a red Mercedes, a green Volvo, a blue sedan, a white SUV – and while this Rolodex is spinning and spinning all around it are thoughts about that time I almost died in a car crash because the front tire in my car exploded as I was speeding around a curve, and then I remember how the side of that car sheared away entirely, and then I am also remembering endless drives in that car around town during empty high-school nights when we would order shawarma and waraq enab and stacked plastic tubs of hummus and moutabel and toum and eat as quietly as we could in someone's living room, so we didn't wake their parents, while the TV schedule finished for the day and an-Našīd al-Waṭanī as-Saʿūdī would play – martial and bright and rousing – and we would all feel lumps in our throats and feel silly for feeling lumps in our throats, then I remember the way we would ride our bicycles around town in the years before we could drive, our knees skinned, our faces bright red in the heat, stopping at the snack bar for Lion Bars and cans of Mirinda, then I remember a time I was a small girl when my family was driving down the winding country roads of Ireland and my mother screamed because there just in front of us a delivery van hit a little girl riding a too-big bike and her small body spun like a star through the air and my parents stopped our car and rushed out to help the little girl while the driver of the delivery van staggered to the curb and I could see that the horror of what he had accidentally done had driven him away and he was quite gone from inside himself, and then, at the very same time as I am remembering this horror, I am also remembering the glories of Ireland, the lilt of its voices, the Irish boy who wore a cowboy hat whenever he rode his pony and swore to me that he would grow up to be a real American cowboy, the fresh-baked bread and fine, salted butter we ate around a scarred wooden table on a stone floor in an old hunting lodge that smelled of wet dog, cigarette smoke, and centuries of damp, and each of these thoughts as they appear bring with them the attendant emotions and visceral sensations that I felt when they were really happening, so that letting them crash over me is to experience them in their totality once again, to drown in their vivid unfolding reality, which is urgent and textured and insists this-is-really-happening-right-here-right-now.

And, I continued explaining to the school therapist, this doesn't just happen with memories but with everyday life as

I'm living it. If I see, for example, a black car coming down the street, I don't just note it drive by, I feel reality split into a nexus of swirling potential as dozens of latent timelines play out in blink-blink-blink rapid-fire succession. The black car coming down the street could jump the curb and crash into the back of that parked taxi, which would surge forward and crash into that old man sitting at the table outside the cafe drinking a cup of tea and reading the newspaper all alone on this cold day, and also the black car could swerve into oncoming traffic and then the street would fill with the teeth-grinding sound of metal crumpling against metal and the police would come and ambulances would come and sirens would paint the cold air blue and blue and blue, and also the black car could rev its engine right in the critical moment between two beats of my heart and the flash-flood of adrenaline would be enough to knock my heart's rhythm off-kilter and I would feel a pain grip my chest and I would stagger into the person next to me clutching at them pulling them down gasping for help, and each of these thoughts, like the swarming memories, dredges up a silt of emotion and bodily response so that I live not a singular life but life in life in life in life.

And, as all of this is unfolding, I told the counselor, there is still the world around me to contend with, whatever it may be at any given moment. There could be, for example, the beat of a bird's wings as it takes off from the nearby curb, each feather-touching-feather a poem that I want to stop and inhale, the sound of high-heels like bullets on the pavement behind me, the feel of the wind against my cheek first cold and then colder, and the bristling dayfall sound of sunlight on leaves. It is all so much, the internal and the external, it is like I have no borders at all; the world isn't something I move through or even something that moves through me, the world simply *is* me too.

When I finished explaining all of this to the school therapist there was a long moment of silence. Her room was a small, closet-like space tucked away on one of the top floors of the university. Just outside was a stuffy hall that served as a waiting room for nervous-looking students and a shelf of brightly colored pamphlets eager to teach students who will never deign to read them how to practice safe sex and not die of alcohol poisoning.

From the direction of the hallway I could hear the muffled sound of someone coughing and a phone ringing. The therapist cleared her throat and put down her pen. She was a small woman, painstakingly thin, with thin eyebrows and thin lips and colorless hair that sheened in the overhead light. She never did find a word to describe the way my mind worked, so she said she would send me on to another doctor who might be able to help. Then she gave me a pamphlet containing phone numbers that I could call in a crisis.

Who, I wanted to ask as she ushered me out of her office, was I supposed to call when every moment of every day felt like a crisis.

Decades later I will learn that autism is associated with a restless, racing mind and an abundant intensity of sensory perception, which is why the world so often felt overwhelming to me. I will learn too that autism is correlated with heightened states of anxiety. Anxiety is, in fact, one of the most common conditions associated with autism, with up to half of all autistic people having a diagnosis of anxiety. The National Autistic Society found that forty-seven percent of autistic people surveyed fell into the severe anxiety category.[24] Some suggest that autistic people experience severe anxiety due to a lifetime of constant stressors, alienation, and trauma, while others contend that autistic individuals are inherently predisposed to anxiety. It appears that neurodivergent minds may spend more time than is typical in deep, internally focused thought, and have difficulty switching away from this mode of thinking. This predisposition to deep thought has the effect of making neurodivergent people imaginative and original thinkers, but, along with hindering tasks associated with executive functions, it could also have the effect of generating rumination, catastrophic thinking, and the resulting heightened depression and anxiety.[25]

At the time, with no understanding of why my world has come unraveled, why I alone among my friends can't seem to function the way I have been taught I am supposed to function, all I know is *theterrorthepanicthefearthehorror* is a daily occurrence, without fail, and every day I think I will die because of it. It will be decades before I finally learn that not everyone experiences the world the way I do: constantly assaulted by sensory input and their own roaring thoughts. At the time, I assume that everyone is experiencing the same thing. I've never been told otherwise; people don't usually spend a lot of time talking about the way they process information from the world around them, so it never occurs to me that there is anything that unusual about my thought process. What I do think is unusual about me, then, is that I, unlike pretty much everyone else I know, am failing at life.

Leaning over the iron railing, gazing down at the Thames, I watch as the dull sun, nearly hidden behind its pallor of clouds, climbs higher in the sky. All around me, London is coming to life – I can feel the city waking up. Within it, I feel like a thorn of the most ugly wrongness. Throughout my childhood I had been told that I acted like a 'crazy' person and that I should be locked up in a mental institution. This oft-repeated message has left me with a terrible fear that at any moment I might lose my grip on reality and be put away forever. During these grey, lonely months of misery in London, I think this fear might be close to becoming a reality. Cities, I know, are comprised of disconnection and rupture, spaces where other stories bleed in, where other realities take hold as others recede, but now it is undeniable that I too am comprised of the same: I have become the site of rupture.

19. Oakville, Texas, USA, 2003

Hundreds of acres of cattle pasture surround the trailer where I live. Winding caleche roads run through them, roads I walk with my dog, Polly, every evening. These roads are flanked by barbed-wire fences, mesquite brush, prickly pears, and prehistoric-looking yucca plants. There are coyotes and rattlesnakes and sharp-fanged javelina. Amid the faded grass, wildflowers send up flames of color – bluebonnets, red paintbrush, and scarlet sage – while fireflies spark in the wind. From the towering live oak trees, cicadas fill the air with their rattling vibrations. The sound of it is so loud that I feel like I'm not just hearing it but I'm walking through it, like the air itself is a thing I must traverse.

I'm living in a town that has more cattle than people, and everything about America strikes me as strange. So far, America is: men in cowboy hats and cowboy boots with guns in holsters on their hips, small white crosses in bright green grass, depictions of fetuses on billboards, jars for spare change next to gas station cash registers to collect donations for sick children in need of medical care, television commercials advising you to ask your doctor about prescription drugs, phone numbers that work and shops that open when they say they will open, late-night infomercials and television shows that do not pause for prayer time, Slim Jims and Frito pie and Funyuns, gargantuan trucks and sex shops on the side of highways, tornado warnings and hail storms, taxis with meters and buses that come on time, homeless people sleeping in cardboard boxes on city streets where there is no litter to be seen, shopkeepers and clerks and waiters and gas station attendants always smiling, people saying they will pray for me, women jogging down the street in sports bras, tampons in every shop, gas stations where I can pump my own gas, parking rules that are enforced, currency that does not, as I had assumed, go up to 500-dollar bills, arguing with my professors when they give lectures on a place called 'the Middle East', football games and tailgate parties, cinemas that do not cut out the nude scenes, Mormons at my door in white shirtsleeves, learning to catch myself before saying rahamkallah or inshallah or bismillah, and people constantly asking me, 'So, where are you from?' and 'Where is that exactly?'

When I was living in London, an American friend introduced me to classic films she couldn't believe I had never seen, like *Sixteen Candles*, *The Breakfast Club*, and *Pretty in Pink*. In these movies, I saw the ritual pageantry of a specific kind of American youth: proms and parties, football games and cheerleaders, which reminded me of another potent talisman of American teenage culture, *Seventeen* magazine. In our school library in Saudi, we got occasional copies of *Seventeen*, but the magazines were censored, with pages missing, and any model displaying bare limbs or cleavage covered in thick white stickers or layers of black marker. But without satellite TV or internet, these magazines were one of the only direct inputs I had from the world of the American teenager, and I studied them avidly.

On screen and on the pages of magazines, I understood America and I thought I knew what it would be like to live there. But, now that I am here, everything is garishly foreign and perplexing. I can never quite shake the feeling that I am just visiting, unable to comprehend that I really live here now. School breaks when I sometimes fly back home to Saudi feel like sanity-saving forays in the real world that always end far too soon. Never before in my life have I felt what is known as culture shock, but here in America I am feeling it every day.

I'm still mired in the anxiety that plagued me in London, still sickened by regular panic attacks that sometimes make the long drive to my university impossible, but I try to make friends anyway. I go to parties in empty pastures, where people get drunk in the middle of rings of parked dually pickup trucks. I quickly learn that my clothes, which had been acceptable in

London, are in Texas seen as decidedly weird. At one of these parties I see my first keg and embarrass myself when I say, excitedly, that it looks just like in the movies. In America, it turns out the movies are nothing at all like real life.

Speaking to my American peers, I often don't know what to say. I have little consensual social currency to draw from, I don't know the right music or TV shows, and the way I pronounce words makes people give one another funny looks and roll their eyes. I quickly banish all Arabic from my vocabulary, and soon after that words like lorry, lift, flat, and bin. There are whole parts of my life that I have learned it is best not to talk about or else people will think I am lying, or, if they do believe me, they think I'm bragging. I quickly learn just how un-American much of my attitude is – from my manners, to the rhythm of my conversations, even the topics I think are appropriate to discuss with acquaintances. Sometimes I still forget not to lean forward and kiss people on both cheeks when I'm introduced, which inevitably leads to assumptions that I'm somehow putting on airs. There is, it seems, always something I do that catches me out, that makes people pause, give me a quizzical look, and then ask where I'm from.

And now that I no longer drink alcohol, thanks to the fact that it induces panic attacks of unusual ferocity, I find it impossible to keep up the party-going that has typified the last several years of my life. In fact, socializing in general has become an onerous chore. I have long since learned that monologuing on my latest topic of interest does not make for scintillating conversation, but when a special interest naturally arises I find myself convinced, every time, that on this occasion it will be different. When another student in one of my classes says something that I know to be inaccurate and doesn't seem convinced when I offer countervailing information, I insist on taking down her email address and later send her a several-page-long explanation, helpfully accompanied by a list of citations for further reading. What I think of as a richly referenced installment of a hopefully ongoing conversation seems to not have been well received, as I never hear back from her. I am starting to wonder if I will ever make a real friend in this odd country. I don't yet know it but soon I will meet the man I will one day marry, finally finding someone who genuinely loves listening to my giddy impromptu lectures and who eagerly asks questions about the things that make my heart skip a beat. In fact, to my astonishment, he will find all of the ways I don't fit in indispensable to what it is he loves about me. For now, though, he is still a few years and many miles away, so I am left bored and lonely in the strange new world of America.

Around this time, I read books about third-culture kids: kids who spend significant parts of their formative years in a culture outside of their passport culture, resulting in an identity that is influenced both by the parents' culture and the host culture. I joke that because both of my parents were third-culture kids, I must be a third-culture kid once removed. In these books I learn that the time when a third-culture kid returns to the passport country, often to attend university, is known as the re-entry process and it is typically the hardest part of the journey. During the re-entry process, many third-culture kids are what is known as 'hidden immigrants' – a term coined by Dave Pollock and Ruth Van Reken to describe a person who externally appears to be the same as everyone around them, while internally they are, in some respects, more like the country in which they spent their formative years, so, back in their passport country, they are in many ways having what is tantamount to an immigrant experience.[26] It is a constant shock, this nation of mine. And, oddest of all, everyone is always asking me if I am happy to be home.

A month after I moved to the States to finish my undergraduate degree, I pulled onto my college campus just as the radio station I was listening to cut into the music to report that something terrible was happening in New York City: a passenger jet aircraft had just struck the World Trade Center.

At first it was described as an accident, but then, a few minutes later, the reporter came back, his voice hollow as a cave, to tell us that another plane had just struck the other tower.

There was silence on the radio then, an echoing gulf of time that served as an acknowledgement of what that second plane meant. Two planes meant this wasn't an accident, two planes meant this was deliberate, two planes meant that for America everything had changed.

Like most Americans, I spent the following days in front of my television. The images from the recovery effort in New York City seared themselves into my mind – the heroic and the heartbreaking. Sometime in the confusing weeks that followed, a teacher at the local high school, hoping to prevent fear from curdling into hatred, asked me to come and talk to her students. I went and I told them about the Saudi that I felt lucky to call home. I told them about its traditions, the beauty of its landscapes, the humor embedded in the culture, the food and the music and the television shows and the way our neighborhood during Eid filled with the smell of fizzling firecrackers and golden-fried sambusa. I told them that in Saudi it is common to make friends simply because of people going out of their way to be hospitable, people who stop on the road to ask if you need a ride, who insist you come to their house for a meal, who spend two hours of their day ensuring you find the address you were looking for. It is a humbling sort of generosity, one that permeates so many interactions in ways I found myself at a loss to fully explain. In the short time I had in front of that class of frightened students, I tried to give as many details as I could – textures and colors and scents and memories – attempting to coax a place that they could only imagine as shadowy and strange into a world that they would know was full of people who were, in many ways, just like them.

When I finished, the students were quiet. They seemed thoughtful. But I was never quite sure what they made of my talk.

I reach the end of the stretch of caleche road that I walk every evening and a wave of fireflies lifts up over the dry grass, blinking their electric messages into the darkness. If I turn left and walk thirty miles I'd come to a small town, and if I turn right and walk thirty miles I'd come to another small town. My university is 100 miles to the north. It is a drive I make three times a week in a car with an engine that the mechanic says is on the brink of going up in flames, or falling out of the car altogether, but I don't make enough money, at my waitressing job at a nearby truck-stop diner, to replace it.

There had been a better job at a steakhouse in another town, but after two weeks I was fired. I've always struggled to remember people's faces, (another trait often associated with autism) and this hindered my ability to remember who ordered what – a necessity at a restaurant with pretensions of being the finest in town. When the manager gave me the news, she gave me a rueful look and told me she was disappointed I hadn't worked out because she had hired me thinking I was smart.

After being fired I drove home in a semi-panic. What was I supposed to do? Did I need to go to the police station and file a report? How long did I have till my residence visa was cancelled and I had to leave the country?

It took me several minutes to realize that I didn't have to leave, that even without a job I was allowed to remain living in the country because I was a citizen. Being seen as someone who belonged regardless of my employment status seemed like a privilege so improbable that it bordered on the absurd. But it still did not make America feel like home. Even after living here for three years, I remain beset by a geographic dysphoria so profound that it makes every day feel like a day lived in the wrong life, like a mistake has been made. But, other than too-brief visits home to Saudi, here I remain.

When I'm not working or going to school, I'm often walking the country lanes with my Polly. She's a speckled grey brilliance of a dog and the best friend I have ever had. My life for the past several years has felt like it has been in free fall, everything has changed and everything keeps changing with no end in sight. Polly, then, has been the still point at the center of my world. She is the one safe, stable place I have. I tell her every day that she has saved me, that she is the reason I am still here. On our evening walks, together we make our way across cattleguards, beneath the shadowed overhangs of gnarled live oaks, across shallow creeks, and through windswept pastures. I feel the need to thread myself into this strange landscape, to keep moving until my body resonates in a sympathetic, familiar way to the world around me. I think perhaps America, and its swaggering mythos of red-white-and-blue that has hung so strangely around my life, obscures the land itself. The land, which holds stories far more ancient than the nation state that now claims it, emerges sometimes in flashes on these walks, but its rhythm feels odd against the soles of my feet, its melody unpredictable. Texas moves me, the tidal roar of its cicadas and its white-tailed deer flying liquid-fast in the dusk makes me feel awestruck and reverential, but it does not yet conjure in me a sense of belonging. To me, Texas feels like the most foreign place I have ever been.

20. Abu Saiba, Bahrain, 2007

At the edge of a dirt road, our compound's gates stand open, blocked from closing by a dense profusion of pale pink oleander. Boughs of white bougainvillea form cumulus clouds along the top of the outer walls, hiding all but a few stray glints of the shattered glass bottles stuck in cement along the top. In another life, the compound was home to a sporting club, but years ago the buildings were broken up into odd, mismatched apartments where ceiling heights change dramatically from room to room, where bathroom showers are garden hoses over floor drains, and where our front yard is an empty swimming pool filled with petals of fallen jasmine.

Every evening after work, my fiancé and I walk our dogs through the compound's maze-like hedges, pausing at the goat pen to watch the gamboling kids, avoiding the stretch of scorched earth where the residents' rubbish is weekly set ablaze, and walking quickly past the fence that adjoins a camel farm, where truculent faces have been known to leer at us, flashing sharp teeth. On these walks, we head for the far corner of the compound, where, just beyond a dusty palm grove, stands a single Dilmun burial mound.

Being back in the Gulf, finally living here again after seven years going to school abroad, is a dream come true. For the past seven years, since graduating from high school in Bahrain and leaving for university, my trips home had been brief – occasional summer holidays and Christmas vacations, where I always arrived with a plane ticket already in hand stamped with a looming exit date. For the entirety of those seven years, when anyone asked what my plans were after university, I would say simply, 'To go home.'

The response to this dream of mine was less than encouraging. No one seemed to think it was realistic. The most they would concede was that maybe in a decade or so, with some professional experience under my belt, I might find a job willing to hire me and provide the visa needed to let me live in the place I considered home. Somehow, though, with a miraculous quickness, my fiancé and I were both offered entry-level jobs in Bahrain. In a mad dash, we packed up our belongings and our three rescue dogs and, with the indispensable support and encouragement of our families, made the move.

The first morning we woke up in Bahrain, I crept out of bed at sunrise, making my way through my friend's house where we were temporarily staying, dodging a litter of pouncing black-and-white kittens, to stand on the patio in the muggy autumn air. The sun was just rising, the sound of traffic on Budaiya highway creeping up to a low drone, when the call to prayer began from a nearby mosque. And, even as I told myself I was entering the realm of hackneyed cliché, the sound of it was so much the sound of home that I couldn't help it: I cried.

After working in riding stables, pubs, and truck-stop cafes, the job that has brought me to Bahrain has made for a difficult transition. It is my first ever office job and it soon becomes obvious to me, and I think to everyone else, that I am not very good at it. To start, there are meetings. Endless meetings where we spend hours debating the nuanced differences between brochures we might send out – one a delicate shade of periwinkle, and the other a slightly more delicate shade of periwinkle. In these meetings we analyze the protocol of all sorts of things, from fonts and text sizes to launch dates and seating plans. Each of these decisions is of the utmost importance, but I cannot make myself understand their nuances or even care about them as much as I know I should, because it all seems so arbitrary and confusingly convoluted. Then there is the never-spoken-of-but-just-as-important protocol of how to navigate the office hierarchy – a hierarchy I wasn't entirely aware existed until a friendly colleague pointed it out.

When I work at events, I sometimes float behind the registration desk. Attendees approach, fresh from the airport, rumpled suits and hair in disarray, eager for someone to answer their questions, soothe their rattled egos, and point them in the direction of whatever they need more – a cup of coffee, or the bathroom. I am eager to help, so eager and smiley that I think I radiate a confidence and competence I do not have. I quickly become flustered trying to answer questions, register participants, and dole out the badges and gift bags and timetables for whatever kind of ticket they have purchased. But working at the registration desk is the kind of job that is seen as so easy that my colleagues often recruit their college-aged kids to do it – the kind of temporary gig that actual children do to earn a bit of pocket money. But this kind of multitasking fries all the circuits in my brain; within an hour I am flushed, sweaty, tongue-tied, and trying to ignore the exasperated looks from co-workers and attendees alike. *COVID Lockdown = relief!*

I'm having particular difficulty with the constant socializing that office life requires, which surprises me because I've always thought of myself as quite good at it. All my life I've enjoyed performing, and up until my autism diagnosis this is what I thought socializing was, but I'm increasingly struggling with the demands of being 'on' all day long. By the end of the day I sometimes struggle even to speak correctly; words simply won't come when I summon them. At the same time, I find myself having difficulty making sense of the words that are said to me. It all seems like noise – harsh, painful, meaningless noise – and to concentrate enough so that the noise is translated into actual words with actual meanings is sometimes impossible. More and more, when the workday is over, I flee the office.

For many autistic people, socializing is something we can superficially apparently do well. But we do this largely by conscious effort. Our understanding of socializing is not instinctual, but something we have learned on an intellectual level. As a child, I studied the way my peers interacted and I read books voraciously to parse the wild permutations of human expression and interaction and figure out why people did what they did, including a massive Miss Manners book that I read and re-read because it offered clear-cut guidelines for every possible social interaction.

This conscious consideration of every aspect of socializing is called 'masking'. Masking is an attempt by an autistic person to appear neurotypical, in order to evade negative comments, suspicion, or even hostility. Some autistics liken it to a survival strategy. Almost everyone, autistic and non-autistic alike, masks to some extent. For non-autistic people, masking is akin to putting their best foot forward, whereas for autistics, whose baseline behavior is further away from what society deems 'normal', masking can feel like an elaborate, extremely draining, high-stakes performance. High-masking autistic people often assume this is what socializing is like for everyone. Until I was diagnosed, that is what I thought. I assumed everyone felt that socializing was a strenuous, over-exciting, exhausting performance. I assumed we all for some reason just hid what we did behind closed doors – the repetitive movements, the blinking and sniffing and swaying and fidgeting. I assumed we all had obsessive interests that we studied compulsively, forensically collating vast reservoirs of knowledge, but that we knew it was embarrassing to talk about, so we just didn't.

This hyper-focused performance is often not a random assemblage of insincere traits but an amplification of genuine aspects of our personality. In fact, when, more than a decade later, I finally learn about autistic masking, one of the first comparisons that comes to my mind is a writer's performance on the page. I am unable to resist comparing masking to the writing of a memoir – showing an unsettled, mercurial self, playing along the hazy border that exists between truth and fiction, understanding that just by picking and choosing what stories we include, and what stories we discard, we are making a conscious performance of the self. I even wonder if masking can be, at times, an artistic choice.

This is not to suggest that masking is a benign act. Yes, masks can serve us well. They can be protective, ensuring we are not ridiculed, or harassed, or, for many autistics, even worse. And masking can open up opportunities in a world that still demands neurotypical norms of behavior. But because many doctors still base autism diagnosis on externally observable behaviors –

relying on evaluation metrics designed by non-autistic people that rarely take into account internal states – autistic people who mask intensely often fly under the radar entirely, leaving them without the self-knowledge or much-needed accommodations that a diagnosis can provide. While high-masking autistic people are frequently told by doctors they could not possibly be autistic because they can, for example, make eye contact or use humor appropriately, what these doctors don't see – and what they often don't think to ask about – is what comes after an autistic person has been masking, like the days of agitation, extreme anxiety, and dysregulation. Many autistic people report that having to mask to get by in day to day life is one of the most grueling aspects of autism, with damaging side-effects that build over time. High-masking is correlated with a whole host of negative consequences, including exhaustion, anxiety, depression, and even an increased risk for suicide.[27] A study has suggested that autistic individuals in general are three times more likely than non-autistics to attempt suicide, while female autistics are eight times more likely to attempt suicide than women who are not autistic.[28]

For me, what comes after a long period of intense masking can feel like the wreckage left behind after a storm. My mind, which was for so long hyper-focused on putting on a performance of socializing, finds it difficult to change course when the socializing is over. This is a form of autistic inertia; change is hard for us even when it comes to our own mental processes. And then there is the racing heart, the frazzled nerves, the inability to think straight or engage in any other activity, and all the physical side-effects of sensory and information overload that commonly appear in the wake of socializing. Autistic minds are believed to process things at a very deep level, which sometimes means our processing takes a significant amount of time. It can therefore take hours for me to recover after a brief exchange, and several days to regain my equilibrium after intense, important exchanges.

When I was a kid, I had reserves of energy that allowed me to hurl myself at the world, a veritable tornado of bossiness, giddiness, and non-stop talking. I used my own overbearing energy to shield myself from the overwhelming sensory input of my surroundings – a living embodiment of the dictum that says the best defense is a good offense. Talking non-stop not only allowed me to perseverate on my latest favorite topic, but it also shielded me from the jagged, darting unpredictability of conversation. During lulls in conversations my mind quickly pulls me back down into the mode of thinking I so enjoy, deep, all-consuming, analytical thought. To be pulled repeatedly out of this space by someone talking to me can feel both disorienting and aggravating. So, to keep myself anchored in the conversation, I prattle on and on.

As I grew up, though, I learned how off-putting this was. Slowly, over the years, I began to notice that other people weren't as dazzled by my performance as I had assumed they were. Actually, a lot of the time, they seemed put off. So I dialed it back and learned to listen more than I talked. Even if I had wanted to still shield myself from the world in the gregarious way I did as a child, as I grew older those energy reserves naturally dwindled away.

By the time I was in my mid-twenties living back in the Gulf – working in a job that I had to succeed at in order to maintain the visa that allowed me to live there – I insisted to anyone who would listen that everything was absolutely wonderful, yet the truth was that I was running on fumes.

At the end of our evening walks in our ramshackle compound in Bahrain, we reach the Dilmun burial mound. Hidden behind a scattering of palm trees and a stretch of dusty grass, the burial mound is a hillock about twelve feet tall, formed of sand and rocks – an outcropping of the necropolis to the south. The vast Dilmun necropolis was constructed over a period of 400 years, more than 4,000 years ago. Situated across the Bahraini archipelago, the eastern shores of Saudi Arabia, and stretching tendrils northward to Kuwait, the Dilmun civilization that erected such impressive tombs for their dead was a power in the Gulf for thousands of years. In Sumerian mythology, Dilmun may have been seen as a paradisical garden, a place where people did not age and where animals did not kill one another. In this, Dilmun is considered by some as a possible origin for the legend of the Garden of Eden. The burial mounds of Dilmun's necropolis were constructed as towers; they only appear as mounds today because of the degradation of time. Inside are chambers containing the remains of the deceased: men, women, and children. Often there are alcoves surrounding the central chamber, containing mortuary gifts, like sea shells, ivory figurines, pottery, and copper weaponry.

With our dogs panting at our feet – Polly, Lobi, Jack, and Volvo – and our ginger cat, Twilah, scampering in the undergrowth, my fiancé and I sit on the crumbling brick wall that runs through the palm grove and watch the sun set across the top of the burial mound. It is due to be excavated soon, so that whatever it contains can be catalogued and preserved, perhaps even being placed in the national museum. With no clue on the nondescript outside of the tomb to hint at who and what is hidden inside, the site holds an air of mystery. Do the remains belong to a man or a woman? What was their life like? Why did they die? Do they have plush, luxurious mortuary gifts, or were they buried with only a few humble tokens? Is there a child, perhaps a small infant laid to rest along the mound's outer wall?

I spend a lot of time thinking about the life of the person buried inside, what made up the activities of their day, what they ate for breakfast, if they fell in love, and what they stayed up at night worrying about. The gulf of time between me sitting here and the life of whoever it was that is now lying as a skeleton in the burial mound can be hard to grasp. That we both lived in the same place, saw the same stars spiraling overhead, felt the same salt-laced wind rolling in off the sea, seems like a perplexing, potent magic. Sitting here, I am always struck by the notion of a place containing two opposite states simultaneously. A word on my tongue: barzakh.

Definitions upon definitions. The Arabic word barzakh generally means isthmus, but it can also mean barrier or partition, words that give rise to the term's deeper connotations. Barzakh is mentioned three times in the Quran: once as the barrier between the living and the dead, an intermediate realm between our world and the hereafter where the spirit is separated from the earthly body, and twice as the barrier between fresh water and salt water, as even when the two intermingle they are believed to retain distinct characteristics. Both metaphysically and corporeally, then, the barzakh conjures both images of interstitial connection and simultaneous separation.

During this first year back in Bahrain my life feels barzakhian in its ability to contain both my wildest happiness and my growing sense of disillusionment. The life that I had thought possible for me is, day by day, revealing itself to perhaps not be as firmly within my grasp as I had thought. When it had all been a vague dream I played in my head during the years I spent at school abroad, my own limitations were something my imagination helpfully disguised behind a fog of wishful thinking. I had always assumed that somehow things would turn out OK once I was back where I belonged. But now that I am here, now that my wildest dreams of returning have somehow come true, things are going wrong in ways that I, as ever, struggle to understand.

21. Khobar, Saudi Arabia, 2017

I stumble out of the car, my vision a ruin of lights that pop and fizzle every time I blink. At the last intersection we'd been stopped behind an SUV flashing its hazard lights because of the intermittent rain, and I have to wait for my eyes to clear before the dark streets of the souq take shape. Overhead, the night sky is thick with clouds and the whole of the world feels spangled with grief. My dog Polly, my best friend for the last sixteen years, has just died. She lived a long, joyful life and I know I couldn't have asked for more, but here in the wake of her death I feel like a plant that has been uprooted. Meaning no longer coheres to the world around me; everything, everything is falling away.

My husband, Cody, and I walk on into the city night, constructing shapes between our bodies and the lights of lamp posts, becoming dark shambling creatures that wind along the pavement. In the midst of the crowd, I spot a father walking with his three little girls, each in a saffron-yellow salwar kameez. Two boys on a bike, one pedaling, the other standing on the struts, weave in and out of traffic, hollering at everyone they see.

We enter a leather goods shop where rows of hand-tooled sandals sweep up the walls to the ceiling and a cobbler sits cross-legged in the corner, surrounded by his tools and stray bits of leather. He introduces himself and then leaves, going across the street to a cafe, and returning with three paper cups of steaming chai.

While we sip the tea, he works a stiff thread through the sole of a shoe and tells us that he left his home in Peshawar twenty-five years ago and has been working in Khobar ever since. When he arrived, he says, the buildings were shorter and there wasn't as much traffic. Describing the shadowy outlines of a city that now seems fantastical and remote, he says sometimes he forgets it is the same city that he remembers from his youth. Time, he says softly, has a way of changing everything you see and everything you thought you knew. As we talk, men filter in and out of the store, bringing belts and wallets in need of repair. We make our purchase – a belt for my husband – and step back into the night.

Most of the people we pass meander slowly down the streets in small groups, enjoying the winter evening. It rained earlier and the excitement of it still shivers through the air. Children slip in and out of doorways, sandals slapping sharp rhythms against the sidewalk. A truck roars past and my abaya catches in its wake, flaring around my knees, and I spin in a circle, pushing it back down. On one corner, a group of men take up half the sidewalk playing a game of karom, flicking the pieces with snapping fingers. We pass a shop plastered in flyers advertising shampoo and nuts, where blonde dolls with sun-bleached faces fill the windows. There is a smell on the street of dinner cooking, maybe from a nearby restaurant or somewhere in one of the flats up above that perch over the shops. There's chicken and garlic and the golden scent of something breaded being fried.

My father grew up in a tiny town further up the coast and, as a child, he viewed Khobar as a booming metropolis. He and his family would take long, un-air-conditioned bus rides whenever they wanted to visit, but it was worth it to reach the city where everything happened first, fastest, and best. He recalls the sweltering summer day he watched as one of the city's first bulk refrigerators was installed, slipping into the shop afterward to marvel at the frigid air. And the day in 1960 when Ethiopian Emperor Haile Selassie came to town, and my father watched as he and King Saud swept by with their gleaming military escort.

Growing up with these stories, and the stories of my mother and grandparents, made for me a Khobar that exists in multiplicity with itself. Wherever I go, I'm never just in the Khobar of today, but in the Khobar of so many yesterdays, my vision marred by the manifold memories. Sometimes, I think I know this city too well to ever experience it directly; instead, I traverse a gauzy assemblage of recollections.

Across the highway, into the other side of the souq, a tinge of sharp-elbowed fervor permeates the sidewalks. In front of a barbershop two men sit on the curb playing the fastest game of chess I've ever seen, their hands slapping the timer in a frenzied blur. A trickle of music seeps out from a vegetable shop. I peek inside – there seem to be more fluorescent light bulbs on the ceiling than actual ceiling – and find a wall-mounted TV showing shaky footage of a festival where men in luminous thobes are dancing the ardah – Saudi Arabia's traditional dance. They shuffle from side to side, janbiya swinging at their hips, to the insistent beat of a drum. Every so often one of them drifts away from the group to talk on his cell phone or take a smoke break. The shopkeeper, a red-and-white gutra perched low on his forehead, gives me a smile, a stick of bristly miswak wedged between his gums. I say, 'Masa' al-khair,' and he presses a hand to his heart and closes his eyes.

On the next block, we find a rug shop where mountains of rugs sprawl across the canopy-covered sidewalk. An Afghani rug hanging by the door shows images of tanks, soldiers, and guns. At the top is an image of the Twin Towers and a date: *9/11/2001*. Below is a stylized map of Afghanistan filled with troops and American flags. Along the bottom it reads: *Long Live American Soldiers!* The shopkeeper sees me looking and leans out to say, 'In Afghanistan, we used to have only three languages: Arabic, Pashto, and Taliban.' He chuckles at his own joke and ducks back inside.

A soft rain begins to fall and we walk on as the street closes in around us, like a bird quieting for the night. And then, there it is: the shop we call the Time Warp Toy Store. Enter and it is 1983. He-Man reigns supreme. Barbie has crimped hair and shoulder pads. I pick up a puzzle, and on the side of the box a stamp reads: *Made in West Germany*. The bounds of temporal reality are useless here; time rolls toward the shop, hesitates, and turns back. Almost unknown to modern kids who prefer the well-worn routes of shopping malls, this toy store is enshrined in the memory of those of us from the older generations, who remember a time when malls were something we had to leave the country to visit.

The shop is owned by a handful of brothers. As a child, a trip to the store was incomplete until one of the old men sitting in the corner laughed at the way you pestered your parents for whatever toy was that month's necessity. They wore dark thobes and were never without a cigarette and thimbleful of steaming tea. Clacking away in their fingers were always prayer beads.

As an adult, my father once purchased a model airplane from the Time Warp Toy Store. When he paid, he laughingly told one of the brothers that when he first saw the toy, thirty years ago, it had only cost four riyals, whereas now the price was twenty-four riyals. Without missing a beat the owner replied, 'If you give me back those thirty years, I'll give you back your twenty riyals.'

Through the dim and cluttered aisles we roam, unearthing treasures from decades past. Here is a kit so you can put together your very own Challenger Shuttle model. Here is Home Office Barbie, Astronaut Barbie, and Totally Hair Barbie. And here is a replica Patriot missile launcher I would have loved to have when I was a child dragging my gas mask to and from school in the wake of the Gulf War.

We pay for our nostalgic purchases and step back outside where we find the rain has been replaced by a cloud of fog that coats the street in a watercolor haze. We head back to the corniche, stepping off the petunia-lined walkway and sinking into the soft white sand. Leaving the caul of memories to the city that looms at our back, we drift away from the glow of streetlights and walk toward the black rolling sweep of the incoming tide. In my all-consuming grief and dizzying disorientation since Polly's death, the world seems painted in shades of terror. Everything seems terribly wrong. As we reach the edge of the water, I realize I am fighting back tears. My husband pulls me close to him and we stand there watching the surging waves.

I wait for the dark field of the sea to rise up toward the sky, fog banking off the waves, rolling down in thick rivulets to fill the streets and wipe them clean of people and cars and the rush of the day. When the sky is full of salt and seaweed and the grinding gnash of currents, when all the detritus of the day and the long night are converging into a single point, I close my eyes and search for the deep seams that run all the way through our tilting desert.

22. Dammam, Saudi Arabia, 2017

Sitting in the waiting room, the press of the outside world coming from beyond the glass wall of window to my right feels loud against me. There are trucks and jets and pedestrians and an expat man in a too-small blue jumpsuit sweeping the gutter. As he sweeps, clouds of dust billow up from around his feet and tattered scraps of candy wrappers twinkle silver in the sun. Sitting around me there are other people, in their own seats, watching the TV, watching their phones, watching me. Every few minutes a phone bleeps at reception and the receptionist answers, 'Allo?'

Eventually, I am taken into a small room off a big hallway where a kindly nurse takes my blood pressure and asks me to step on a scale, asks me what is the reason for my visit, and then asks me to return to the waiting room, where I sit again on the saggy couch. I count a dozen more 'Allos?' and watch the man in the too-small blue jumpsuit finish the gutter and move on to the sidewalk before I am once again called to follow a different nurse down the big hallway.

In another small room, I find the psychiatrist. He is sharp angles and long arms and he sits with his hands tightly folded in his lap as if prepared for me to deliver bad news. When he asks me what is the reason for my visit, I falter. In so many aspects of my life I have been so fortunate that it feels almost obscene to acknowledge any struggle. I know that to do this I will have to chronicle my life's most challenging chapters, to perseverate on the negative to the exclusion of the good that should rightfully be included. But, if there is indeed an illuminating pattern to be found, I can see no other way.

When I finally begin, I say the reason for my visit is the barrage of racing thoughts that are eating me alive, the reason is the panic that shadows my every waking moment, the reason is that meditation only helps the way it would help maintain equanimity while your face is being slapped, the reason is my inability to straightforwardly do things – work in an office, run errands, go out to dinner, go on holiday – that so many other people seemingly do with ease, the reason is my inability to adjust to the smallest change in plans or routine without feeling a throbbing sense of wrongness so disorienting and painful it sometimes makes me think that life might not be worth living, the reason is the sound of all of the world's electricity and the rough rasp of a cat licking her paws and the tick tick tick of a cooling AC unit, the reason is that when my thought process is interrupted it feels like a grenade has been tossed in the center of my skull, the reason is the way I blink and blink and blink and sniff and sniff and sniff and sway and sway and sway, the reason is the shattered language that flies from my mouth making sense only to me, the reason is the way I take things literally and so often miss other people's sarcasm, the reason is the bliss I feel when I am studying the topics that I love more than I can describe, the reason is that I try so hard to make friends but never quite manage, the reason is all my life people calling me weird, the reason is a lifetime in therapy for my struggles to only intensify, the reason is that my compassion for animals sometimes makes it hard to leave the house because the sight of another guileless pigeon crushed in the street makes it impossible for me to breathe, the reason is the jittery exhaustion I feel after socializing that can leave me jagged for days, like my thoughts have been replaced by a whirlwind of broken glass, the reason is the cascade of thoughts always in my head, a swirling maelstrom where everything I see or hear or smell or remember brings with it a host of associated thoughts, which in turn bring their own hosts of associated thoughts, which in turn bring their own hosts of associated thoughts, until my mind feels like it has the coherence of a sandstorm.

When I am done speaking the doctor unfolds his hands. He asks me follow-up questions and makes notes in his folder. He hands me a box of tissues and that is when I realize I have been crying. When the words 'autism spectrum disorder' are spoken they are only a string of syllables that falls to the floor. He tells me that he doesn't know of anyone that he can refer me to that evaluates adults for autism, so I would have to pursue further evaluation on my own.

'But even if you were officially diagnosed,' he says, holding his office door open for me to leave, 'there are very few support options available for adults. After all, you already know how to carry on a conversation, so what more do you even need help with?'

23. Dhahran, Saudi Arabia, 2020

The neuropsychologist begins his questions immediately.

We cover my entire life, from my earliest memories to what I did just yesterday. When did I speak, when did I walk, when did I learn to read, did I have seizures, did I have allergies, did I have unusual habits or hobbies, did I have tics? Never before has a doctor pressed so hard, asking questions so rapidly, questions that are intensely intimate, that pull out aspects of my life so embarrassing that I have never shared them with anyone, let alone a stranger with a pen and a clipboard to record all the humiliating details.

But, as soon as I have admitted to some weird quirk or inexplicable thought, I am presented, whiplash quick, with a cognitive test complete with a ticking clock hurrying me along. He asks me to reveal the strange sounds I make and the rhythmic patterns I create with my hands, and I oblige, face flaming, and then the next moment he asks me to reel off all the animals I can think of that start with 'E', before moving on to ask me to describe my checking rituals – front door, back door, oven, dishwasher, washer, dryer, AC, dog's water bowl, back gate – before asking me to describe in more detail the stuttering confusion, anger, and discomfort that overcomes me when a conversation changes subject before I am ready to let something go. Then he asks me to describe the ever-increasing difficulties I face with socializing and the dysregulation and exhaustion that comes after, and then gives me a confusing attention exam in which I have to click and click and click and click and click and click at a computer keyboard at every appearance of a flashing dot on the screen until suddenly the dot doesn't appear and I am not supposed to click anymore, but my inexorable mind keeps my finger click-click-click-clicking. Before I can guess how badly I am doing, he is asking me to recite the details I can remember from a story he read to me twenty minutes earlier about a man with a hat and a lost wallet. He then asks me to elaborate on the eruption of anxiety that derails my life, the gnawing madness of flashing lights or background chatter or tight collars, and he asks me to explain exactly why it was that I was able to succeed in graduate school when I attended virtually, rather than in person. Then he wants to know more about my childhood, then there is another cognitive test with shapes that I must mentally spin and place in the correct order, and then and then and then, there is always something else, another question, another test, another intimate thought to reveal, until it feels that I have been completely turned inside out.

The assessment lasts for six hours. It is designed to push me beyond my limits to see if, in those moments of exhaustion and confusion, something significant will be revealed. It feels as if all of my life is being funneled into this narrow moment in time so that each beat of existence can be grabbed around the neck and held still by rough hands, its fur examined, its fangs peered at, its eyes pulled wide by prying fingers to see what there is to see.

When the assessment is over, I shut down in the most dramatic fashion. I leave my body, I exist somewhere else, I watch all from afar. For three days I barely speak and I barely think and I barely listen. I lie in bed and stare at the same page of the same book. There is an emptiness within me that is unnatural and eerie, like an exposed beach before a tsunami.

I meet the neuropsychologist again at the follow-up appointment to get my results, and again we begin immediately. Within a few sentences, he informs me that I am autistic.

I am autistic and he relays this information neutrally.

I am autistic and he guides me through the seventeen-page assessment results.

I am autistic and he explains why he and the other evaluating doctors made the diagnosis.

I am autistic and when he says goodbye, he wishes me luck.

24. Khobar, Saudi Arabia, 2020

In the wake, I walk.

In the wake, asphalt meets heel and rings like a bell through bone.

In the wake, I speak the street to myself, measuring out the vibrato of its arterial surge. The city is the same city that it was yesterday, which is to say it is an entirely new beast.

In the wake, I do not think human thoughts in the city but thoughts of concrete and coral stone. I bury myself in the sand beneath the city as I walk, threading out to find the fault lines of this artificial shore, dreaming the dreams of the once-coral reef and the once-seabed and the once-gurgle of an underwater aquifer.

In the wake, I go backward in time and sift through my life for the border that is me and the border that is autism, wondering if there even is a border, or if I will scrabble with my fingers for wood that feels like stone and stone that feels like wood, finding only memories of untouchable history laced with fast-flying spears. It is anything but fixed, the story of the self, and this new word I have been given to describe me seems to slip and slide out of my grasp.

In the wake, I think of my husband, who has believed me to be autistic since the word first floated cloud-like into the air as a possibility. To him, it was abundantly evident that here was a story that included me, a story that was, in fact, worthy of celebration. With his help, I begin to let myself experience what it means to be storied in this way and, in the wake, bolstered by this new understanding, things that did not make sense, things that never made sense, suddenly do.

I list the words the city speaks again and again: yellow because always yellow, the flap-filament of a broken dress, dirty globules of spit threading the way, ginger on ginger on puce, a spackle of fragments upside the hand, the heft of a glittering bank, the might of a concrete dais, the posters and the posters and the posters from Eid and the Eid before and the Eid before the Eid before.

I study the stories that pass my way, studying most closely the ones that hesitate and linger, the ones that refuse to be definitively one thing or the other.

In the wake, I walk. Unmoored, ungraspable, I drift even as I drift.

25.

Arianna Dagnino describes dispatriate transcultural writers as 'liquid people, fluid characters flowing in their stories as much as they do their lives.'[29] We are, according to her, hard to grasp.

Hard to grasp, I contend, because, native to the interstice, we see the interstice everywhere, even inside ourselves. We are, more than anything, porous.

The Gulf is a porous, temporary, leaking home to millions, and, because foreigners in the Gulf tend to remain foreigners, most of us will one day leave. For these millions, the Gulf is a porous home/not-home, a place to live out a life of not-quite-belonging.   Transcultural / mixed families?

Liquid people learn liquid tricks. In this place of convergence and separation, full of holes and liquid people, we slip through, like liquid pouring through fingers. Our eyes riven with interstice, we learn new ways of seeing. We gather up new tongues and new customs, wear new costumes that fit like better skins. Fed by the flows of various cultural predispositions, we form identities that are as unpredictable as they are ostensibly strange. We become what we were not and, because our becoming is perpetual, we become the cumulation, the forward motion, the spreading borders of the interstice. For us, the Gulf is a home that we are just passing through.

26. Seef, Bahrain, 2019

Walking at the edge of the city, I watch the green glass face of the sea. Motorized dhows slice across the waves, heading into the setting sun. The evening is dimpled with light and the feel of the humid air is aquatic.

The shore has expanded since the last time I saw it because a new landscape is being summoned from its depths. There is now a building site here with the skeletal gleaming of a some-day hotel. As on the many construction sites dotting this city, there are men everywhere on this patch of rocky sand, carrying tools, driving heavy machinery, and scaling scaffolding, so that I must look up and up and up to follow their path. These men, expatriates who have come from India, Bangladesh, Pakistan, Sri Lanka, and Nepal, build the cities of the Gulf.

The Gulf's expats make up roughly half of the region's population, and within the Gulf the bounds between citizen and foreigner can be vigorously demarcated, linguistically, sartorially, and spatially. Defining what one is in relation to what one is not – or *who* one is not – is not unique to the Gulf, of course: it has been a defining feature of humankind throughout our history and is evident in all modern nation states. In this regard, the stories that we think are remarkable about the Gulf are, in truth, stories that are repeated all over the world.

And, all over the world, in the stories that are told about the Gulf, the romanticized iconography of the tribal Bedouin past takes preeminence. Thus, the Gulf's myriad forms of cultural, ethnic, and religious identity, can, to the unfamiliar observer, appear oversimplified. This thread of the Gulf's story, taken on its own, can reinforce misconceptions that the Gulf was once culturally homogenous, that before the advent of the oil age there was no one here who wasn't *from* here. But, as Neha Vora writes:

> Indian Ocean historiographers have traced vast networks of communication, travel, and exchange between Asia, the Middle East, Africa, and the Mediterranean back to before the arrival of oil or European presence. These works highlight kinship networks, religions, and languages that stretch across continents, indicating that the pre-oil cultures of the Gulf and coastal South Asia were anything but homogenous [. . .][30]

What is new, then, is not a cosmopolitan Gulf society, but the notion that it was ever anything but.

In the Gulf today, most foreigners are here because of the labor they provide, or because they are related to someone who is providing labor. This carries with it the understanding that when this labor can no longer be provided they must leave. In the Gulf, nationality can determine what job a person is eligible for, what pay they will receive, where they can live, what kinds of cars they can buy, and whether they will be allowed to bring their family with them when they relocate. In Gulf cities, as in most cities, there are overlapping worlds. Even when we are in the same place, we are occupying different spaces, moving differently through the city, being perceived differently in the city, making the city even as it makes us. In the Gulf, there are social clubs that cater to different nationalities – Indian Clubs, British Clubs, Pakistani Clubs, and there are schools that do the same – Chinese schools, Indian schools, American schools, British schools, French schools, Pakistani schools, and so on. In both clubs and schools, traditions from the passport country are kept alive: national flags fly, the history of a faraway land is taught, and children are kept oriented toward the fact that one day they will leave and return to the place they are told is home. Adding to this there is the bureaucratic necessity for foreigners to maintain their employment visas and make sure their paperwork is always in order, all of which, as Khaled A Abdulkarim suggests, means that part of the fundamental makeup of everyday life that informs many Gulf expats' sense of self is the constant awareness of their own impermanence.[31]

And yet, somehow, roots. Willful, contrary, they grow. For some of us, especially those of us born here, the roots already reached deep, heart-dark soil before we were old enough to consider whether or not this was wise. It is because of these roots that when I need to describe myself in a professional capacity I tend to say that I am a writer from the Gulf. I wasn't always so direct about it, though. I used to pad my bio with equivocation, fearing that the truth was too weird to state so bluntly. I would throw in the term third-culture kid, or find other filler words that were technically factual but served only to put distance between what I was saying and the truth.

It was seeing the author Deepak Unnikrishnan describe himself simply as 'a writer from Abu Dhabi' that gave me the push needed to drop all equivocation. Unnikrishnan, whose family is from India, was raised in Abu Dhabi. When I saw him describe himself as *from* Abu Dhabi, with no hedging, no explanation, it had a profound impact on me. I had never seen an expat from the Gulf do that so bluntly before, and, in its simplicity and its refusal to quibble, it was radiant. Unnikrishnan writes that he began to describe himself this way because:

> I needed people to know I had roots in the Arabian Peninsula. That people like me – children of the transient diaspora the Gulf cultivated – nonchalant about allegiance and flags, counted and existed. That within the confines of some of our own homes, the only heirlooms left were the stories.[32]

In *Temporary People*, Unnikrishnan's 2017 novel about the South Asian 'guest worker' community in the United Arab Emirates, where eighty percent of the population are expatriates, he explores the inherent strangeness of this in-between existence – unsettling simplistic understandings of belonging, identity, and home. In stories woven across 'chabters', construction workers transmogrify into luggage, ideal expatriate workers are grown artificially in labs, and the tongue of an English-speaking boy who goes to an Indian school in Abu Dhabi leaps from his mouth and brings chaos to the city streets, reveling in the polyphonic exuberance of transculturality.

Unnikrishnan reveals what a potent lens magical realism is to explore transcultural identity within a Khaleeji context. The Arabian Gulf is a region marked by rapid change, where the horizon can shift on a monthly basis as new buildings spring up, where the population of whole neighborhoods can transform in a year, and where the ground beneath your feet can change as the coastline is pushed out through land reclamation projects. The Gulf is a place that can feel permanently in flux and lends itself to fantastical portrayals. By deftly undoing the reader's conception of what is possible, magical realism asks questions about the very nature of our experience: whose reality is real? Whose version of events is accurate? What story lives closest to what truth?

Unnikrishnan's stories – which abound with characters who transform into suitcases, or birds, or even jetliners – emphasize the shape-shifting tendency inherent in transcultural identity. In these tales, the Gulf is both a land of longed-for opportunity and simultaneously a land of homesickness and loneliness. With their elastic realities, these stories have the space to hold these permutations of experience that do not contradict one another but inform one another, reflecting what Vora describes as the 'multiple logics of belonging and citizenship' that exist within the Gulf.[33]

In a global system increasingly premised upon the drifting of people, it is perhaps the privileged few who can experience the resulting rootlessness as a good thing. For many, it is something that must be done simply to survive. The resulting sense of displacement is not then something to be enjoyed, but something to be endured. An acquaintance of mine came to the Gulf from Kerala twenty years ago to work as a groom at a riding stables. He does not call the Gulf home, but he does look pensive when he describes the way he feels now when he goes back to Kerala. It is not about place, he says, but time. Time is what you lose: the feel of time making sense. It feels like things should not move on when we are gone from the place where our heart lives, he says, but they always do.

When one day I leave the Gulf, even if it feels like things should not move on when I am gone, I know they will. There will be new neighborhoods that I will never see, new plazas and parks that I will never visit, new feelings on old streets that I will never know. The people that build these places will one day be gone too, carrying stories of a place they once knew, a place that, for some of us, may have felt like home.

27.

I tell no one about my diagnosis.

It is unwieldy, a rogue planet spinning through space with too much gravity. Even as I find myself acknowledging how well it explains my life, how perfectly it fits, the stories in my head still contain too many of the old stories about what autism is, and it seems they are reluctant to release their grip.

28. Manama, Bahrain, 2018

Where, in centuries past, dhows scudded to shore, laden with teak and silk and gold, there is now a roundabout of idling taxis, their drivers balancing paper cups of karak on their knees, misbaha swaying from rearview mirrors. On a wall by an electronics store is a spray of graffiti in potent indigo: a heart wearing a crown of fire. At the street corner is a censer of burning oud billowing smoke into the faces of passersby. The worst of the day's heat has finally relented and the souq is filling with throngs of slow-moving people, honking cars, and swerving bicycles.

The narrow lanes of the souq tangle and double back because Manama grew haphazardly over the centuries with each new wave of immigration. Nelida Fuccaro writes that the Manama of the nineteenth century was a profoundly transcultural city full of merchants, travelers, and newcomers, tightly linked to international trade networks.[34] In this setting, languages themselves were manifold – Arabic, English, Farsi, Hindi, Sindi, Gujarati, Persian, and more were all swirling through its winding streets.

The polyglot and multicultural nature of Bahrain is evident in the souq today. There are Bangladeshi tailors, Nepalese restaurants, Gujarati restaurants, Keralan restaurants, Iraqi ice-cream parlors, Persian tea houses, and American burger chains, all crowded together in these blocks. Walking by a coffee shop whose benches spill onto the sidewalk, I hear conversations in Arabic, Malayalam, and Farsi, the languages blending into an aural fog of lilting consonants and cascading vowels. Advertisements on nearby shop windows join the multilingual chorus, listing wares in Arabic, Urdu, English, and Tagalog. It seems that no one here, not even the shop windows, is monolingual.

Spoken by more than 400 million people, Arabic is the fifth most commonly spoken language in the world, but, for non-native speakers, it can be incredibly difficult to master. The Arabic that I speak, gathered from friends, television, haphazard classroom study, and my father – who grew up speaking the local dialect fluently and studying Classical Arabic throughout his education – is an odd mix. Unpolished, shambolic, and far too rudimentary for me to claim that I speak it with any skill, talking in Arabic is nevertheless something that pulls at me in curious ways, helping me make sense of what it means to be a liquid person from the Khaleeji interstice.

Arabic is the language of Islam. Within a hundred years of the advent of Islam in seventh-century Arabia, Muslim armies had conquered vast swathes of Africa, the Middle East, and Europe, and would go on to establish some of the largest empires in history, which were to eventually range as far east as China and as far west as Spain. As Max Rodenbeck notes, this globe-spanning conquest brought the Arabic language onto the world stage, where it would come to rival Latin and Greek in its scope and significance as a storehouse of humanity's knowledge.[35] The sweeping legacy of Arabic is evident today in the language's dialectal terroir. A diglossic language, one variety of Arabic is used in formal writing and certain speaking situations, while another variety operates in parallel for everyday communication. There is such a wide variation in this vernacular Arabic – a phenomenon known as a dialect continuum – that people at opposite ends of the continuum can find it challenging to communicate because their versions of the language are so different. Moroccan Arabic, for example, has traces of Berber, while Levantine Arabic has elements of Aramaic. Here in the Gulf, Arabic is rich with the influence of Persian and Hindi. And Arabic has left a legacy in many European languages, owing to the centuries of Islamic rule in the Iberian Peninsula: Portuguese, Catalan, and Valencian all retain words of Arabic origin, while Spanish alone has thousands of words derived from Arabic. Even English contains an array of Arabic-origin words, words that pop out at me when I'm reading, like apricot, algebra, caravan, elixir, lime, nadir, serendipity, sofa, zenith, and zero.

Walking on, I pass the dim hulk of an old mall – once the only shopping mall on the island, where people came to shop for boots and bishts and good silver jewelry. Now, though, people go to the new malls on the coastline and, left all alone, this shopping center dreams the lonely dreams of concrete and cement. In the shop windows, the mannequins watch me with their walleyes, remembering me last year, the year before that, and all the years of my life, all the way back to when I was a child staring up at them when they were new and racy in their bare-skinned perfection. I would run my fingers across the writing on their windows, tracing out the words in Arabic and English, melding the two together in my mind to speak into existence an entirely new language, a dialect born between my tongue and my teeth, a thing entirely my own.

On the next street, I pass two girls throwing rocks at a satellite dish, a woman using a broom to beat dust out of a faded rug, and a pack of off-duty US servicemen with their shorn hair, big backpacks, and nervous eyes. I pass a dumpster overflowing with moldy mangoes, and a fabric store draped in clouds of polyester and silk. I pass a neat white mosque whose outer walls are covered in a mural of bright, childlike figures with sunny faces. I pass a narrow lane spangled with garlands of jasmine and marigold, where I see the 200-year-old Shri Krishna Temple, the oldest Hindu temple in the Gulf. Inside the courtyard, beneath a towering banyan tree, is a flock of nearly tame pigeons, their coos quilting the air. Somewhere in the blocks around me is the Gulf's only official Jewish synagogue, and a few blocks to the south is the small church in which my husband and I were married. Everywhere my gaze settles something grabs my attention – graffiti in Arabic, a poster in English, a shop sign in Urdu – like a swirl of voices clamoring for me to pause, to look, to consider.

The Manama souq is often described as a mosaic of cultures but 'mosaic', with its connotation of strict delineations between separate entities, isn't right. It doesn't capture the reality of transcultural space. Cultures, after all, are not distinct, homogenous units but currents of influence that continually overlap and transform with every interaction. In places like the souq, thrumming with hybrid currents, cultural markers pop and flare: a frazzled, henna-dyed beard; an ankle-skimming thobe; a red-and-white gutra high upon the head, cobra style; a crumpled Nehru jacket; the sinuous coil of a turban. The pops of information brought on by the beard, the thobe, the jacket, they could all mean what I think they mean. Or, they could all mean something – anything – else.

Familiar with this place, one understands how many different ways there are to be fluent, ways that go beyond spoken language. There is cultural fluency, being multilingual in the way of bodies, knowing how to bend and slide around the beliefs of others, to make ourselves spacious and ephemeral. To find comfort in being misunderstood and familiarity in not understanding, to seek spaces where things are not yet solidified, where they are still cohering, where new

83

connections can be made. According to Mikhail N Epstein and Ellen E Berry, at a cultural level this outward-looking evolution is vital, for on their own cultures are inherently incomplete.[36] Unlike multiculturalism, with its essentialist demarcations that can lead to an over-emphasis on difference, Epstein and Berry suggest that a transcultural approach can orient us toward an exploration of the lush potential of the interstitial zones of cultural overlap, as well as allow for individual freedom when it comes to the formation of cultural connections. In this view, cultural interaction is not seen as a chance to homogenize, as in the flattened banality of globalization, but as a process of potent diversification. We can then not only ask what our culture is becoming, but what we ourselves are becoming.[37] As Wolfgang Welsch suggests, when we allow individuals to fully claim the multiplicity of their cultural identities rather than forcing them to choose one or another, we open the path for cultures at large to do the same.[38]

I feel at home in the souq, when I am moving down these narrow streets with their conflagration of tongues and these alleys that gulp great mouthfuls of salty wind from the nearby sea. However, my feeling of belonging, contrary to what many may assume, is not suffused with a presumptuous yearning for things to change so that I may remain here forever. There is a barzakhian logic to this. Within a barzakh, boundaries are necessary. Cultures – and the self, and much more besides – are inherently dynamic, but acknowledging this is not to view all change as something to be automatically pursued in thoughtless haste. That would be evidence of a mentality of flatness, of plastic sameness and crude efficiency that seeks to steamroll over the living texture of earthbound roots. We are embodied beings, which means that the parables sown by limits are intrinsic to our deepest rhythms. It is, in fact, understanding the transcultural aspects within myself and within cultures at large that has, perhaps paradoxically, made me more able to recognize the value in maintaining a supple connection to the past informed by an understanding of the necessity of the edge. Edges are often essential, boundaries frequently serve a purpose, and knowing the stories behind them makes them harder to thoughtlessly dismiss. The way I feel at home here in the souq is bound by limits that by their very existence highlight how precious a feeling it is to belong. Boundaries are often the places where friction is created and where differentiation blooms, and both are necessary ingredients for new stories to emerge – and for old stories to be understood in a new light.

I also feel at home when speaking my slantways Arabic, when I become different from myself, a strange new person falling through language, incandescent. Transcending the foibles of my flummoxed tongue, the beauty of the Arabic language engulfs me, so that sometimes I feel overwhelmed by it, repeating words or phrases under my breath until it seems that I never knew any other consonants but these. I feel stolen away by its rules of grammar, often transposing them to English, confusing my husband, making myself laugh. The language moves through me, or rather, I move through it, discovering different parts of myself, inhabiting different thoughts, finding space where there had not been any space before.

As the alleyways purple with shadow and the shopkeepers toss faded sheets over tables of unsold fruit, I trace my steps back through the narrow lanes, passing halwa shops, karak cafes, silversmiths, and tourist shops filled with enticement. The air is riverine, thick with the scents of cigarette smoke, frying onions, scalded milk, and cardamom. I drink a paper cup of karak chai as I walk, the silt of spices tingling my tongue, and find my way toward the edge of the souq, toward the streets that lead to the highways and the coast and the churn of the sea.

At the mouth of one lane I find a mirror. Chipped and cracked along the bottom corner, it has been sat out for the rubbish collectors to take away. I walk by it and watch my reflection ripple, buckle, then right itself. I recall the Arabic word for mirror, the word for myself, the word for all-alone-in-this-heat-struck-evening city. Standing there, watching the rippling stranger in the glass, I am reminded of something Arianna Dagnino writes:

> Flowing within the confluence, within the transcultural continuum, the individual gradually realizes that the Other is not an enemy, not a stranger, not an alternative, and most of the time not even an Other, but just a mirror of the various possible faces, the multiple understandings of human existence, the varied definitions of belonging that can be grasped, refuted, or internalized. We must look into this mirror, not to lose ourselves in confusion, but to see our selves, our options, and our choices with greater clarity.[39]

29.

A year has passed and still I tell no one about my diagnosis because what if no one believes me? Reading accounts from other late-diagnosed autistic people, I see this is a common concern. And, for some, it is justified. Before a diagnosis, many autists were chided for their strange ways, for not being able to get it together, for being too sensitive, too weird, too intense. Yet, after a diagnosis, autists are often met with skepticism and by people telling them they are too normal to possibly be autistic.

I find many accounts online of women who were diagnosed in mid-life after experiencing autistic burnout, which is a veritable implosion of life. Caused by periods of intense stress, change, or by the cumulative effect of a lifetime of trying to live up to neurotypical expectations, autistic burnout is characterized by long periods – sometimes months, sometimes years – of debilitating exhaustion and heightened sensory sensitivity, often accompanied by a loss of skills and ability to cope with routine life demands, and with concomitant anxiety and depression. Reading these accounts I finally think I know what has been happening in my life over the past few years since Polly died, and why I was finally diagnosed.

I know that those of us who mask intensely are especially likely to be met with, at the very least, confusion when we share our diagnosis. I can't even imagine revealing to people all of the things I've spent a lifetime concealing – the tics, the echolalia, the inability to function in a 'normal' way. I have been taught all my life that these traits are shameful and embarrassing, and I have also been taught that seeming needy or wanting attention, or, even worse, wanting help, is one of the worst things a person can do. The fact that I know none of these things to be true when it comes to other people doesn't touch the intensity with which I feel them to be true when it comes to myself. And so I tell no one and continue on in a murky space defined by dizzying contrasts: flashes of light that illuminate and explain so much of my life, interspersed with epochs of dense darkness that feel like embarrassment and shame.

30. Muharraq, Bahrain, 2018

I walk through a matrix of words. Muharraq, once the capital of Bahrain, is a web of coral-stone alleyways where the buildings run together in uninterrupted sinuous streams. It is prayer time and the layer of voices falling from the neighborhood's mosque minarets form a dense weave of language that thickens the air. Walking, I can feel the vibrations tunneling into me. Walking, I can feel the words passing through gristle and bone, gathering in my gullet, the rhythm calibrating a sameness in my tides.

The morning began on a boat. Leaving from the National Museum on the Bahraini archipelago's main island, the boat carried me across green waves fizzing with foam, spackled with sun, rough with chop, and deposited me at Bu Maher Fort, the starting point of Bahrain's Pearling Path. Squat, stone, and lapped by waves, the fort was empty. The coastguard base I could see over the wall was hectic and modern and shrill, there were horns and shouts of activity, but nearer the fort, with its pale ochre walls and collection of swaying palm trees, I found patches of shade and quiet. It felt like an outcropping from an other time, the shadows dappling the shore felt insubstantial and remote. Despite periods of being submerged underwater, the spit of land that guards the entrance to Muharraq Bay shows archeological evidence of having been the site of fortifications for centuries, possibly millennia. In years past, it also served as the traditional launch point for pearl divers as they set out in fleets of dhows for the summer pearling season.

Entering the glass-walled visitor center next to the fort, I find the air-conditioned air shockingly chill and the place utterly silent. Summer in the Gulf is a time when anyone who can, local and foreigner alike, flees to cooler climes, leaving those of us who remain to roam the temporarily empty cities. I have the place to myself.

In the center of the room there is a sleek diorama depicting a map of the Pearling Path. The serial heritage site comprises seventeen restored buildings dotted along a three-and-a-half kilometer pedestrian path in one of Muharraq's oldest neighborhoods, and is designed to offer visitors an insight into Bahrain's long pearling history. The dual waters that give Bahrain (which in Arabic means 'two seas') its name, fresh water and salt water, are thought to contribute to Bahrain's uniquely lustrous pearls, which are considered the finest in the world. Before oil, pearling was one of the dominant industries in the region and Bahrain's pearls brought the Kingdom fame and fortune for centuries

A museum attendant emerged from a doorway and asked if I needed any help. I said no, but then, impulsively, told her I was going to walk the whole of the Pearling Path today.

Her concern was immediate. 'But it's not finished yet,' she said, coming closer. 'The restorations are not complete.'

'I know,' I answered, immediately feeling guilty for saying anything. She looked genuinely worried that I would be disappointed. I told her that I wanted to see how the path was right now, still undone and burgeoning, but she did not seem convinced.

Once I left the museum I crossed a highway busy with construction trucks and taxis on their way to the airport. Then, for a time, I lost myself down residential streets, each one feeding into the next without an opening between the buildings, funneling me further from where I wanted to be. Eventually, the street narrowed into an alley that came to a dead end. There were windows behind wrought-iron bars and a gate topped with crushed glass and straggly vines of jasmine. A white cat panting in a puddle beneath a dripping AC unit watched me as I turned to retrace my steps.

Millenia ago, Muharraq was the site of an ancient order who worshipped a shark god named Awal, and for a time that was the name of the island itself. This name appears today in the faded signs I see as I make my way back toward the path I was meant to be on, used as a brand name for all sorts of businesses. By the time I find Al Ghus house, a low blocky building with a tall palm tree in its central courtyard, the sun is high in the sky. Inside, I find a small house restored to show the kind of home a pearling captain might have lived in. More comfortable than the barasti huts the divers would have lived in closer to the shore, this home is nevertheless humble, with only a few small rooms.

Wealthier than the captains were the pearl merchants, the tawawish, who owned fleets of pearling boats and financed pearling expeditions. Traders came from all over the world, from India to France, to sit in the majlis of their shops to select their choice of Bahrain's legendary pearls. The tawawish built grand coral-stone homes that had multiple courtyards and tall wind towers, all decorated with finely detailed plaster carvings.

For generations, life in Bahrain revolved around the pearl, with much of the population working as boat builders, pearl divers, doctors who treated divers' maladies, pearl traders, or sellers of the provisions the dhows needed for their voyage. Bahrain's pearls were famous for thousands of years, not just for their luminous beauty but for their medicinal properties too. It was believed by some that if crushed and consumed, Bahrain's pearls could restore one's youthfulness. This even made Gulf pearls a feature in an ancient Mesopotamian legend, *The Epic of Gilgamesh*, one of the oldest known stories in human history.

But by the end of the 1920s, Bahrain's pearling economy was in tatters due to the introduction to the world market of Japanese cultured pearls. Grown easily, in predictable conditions that didn't require risky months at sea and lung-busting dives, Japan's cultivated pearls were relatively inexpensive and reliable, and they wiped out global demand for traditional pearls. Bahrain's economy was thrown into turmoil, so much so that the wider Gulf economy was destabilized.

For Bahrain, everything would change once again in 1932, when, at the foot of Jebel Al Dukhan – the mountain of smoke – oil was discovered. A year later, the oil field – named Awali, after the ancient god – was gushing in commercial quantities. This set off a frenzy of exploration in the region as additional fields were sought – and found. Oil, and the wealth it brought, could not have come at a more fortuitous time, and stories spread throughout the Gulf, and beyond, that Bahrain was an island where a man could make his fortune.

When the heat of the day is too intense, I step into the cool, dim air of Ahmed's workshop to learn about the songs of the pearl divers. The workshop smells of wood shavings and varnish, and the walls are crowded with posters of Ahmed and his band, who play at weddings and Eid celebrations. Ahmed, along with his many sons and grandsons, also makes traditional instruments by hand. He is a short, stout man with bristling red hair, round eyes behind thick glasses, and when he talks he pauses for long stretches, as if savoring the silence. Right now, he is chatting to me with his body half-buried in a crowded closet. When he reappears he is bearing a fat-bellied drum.

'This type,' he says, settling it against his torso, 'long time ago is from East Africa. You make it tighter by heating the skin, or rubbing with grease.'

He patters on it with his fingers to show me its light, sharp tone. The sound reminds me of high school, when the boys at the back of the class would join together in a volley of darboukeh, hands flying against their desks, ignoring the teacher's cries of disapproval.

Grabbing a set of drums, Ahmed rattles out another beat. 'The tabla. From India,' he says, between percussive pops. He gives his hips a shimmy. 'Good for dancing.'

Behind the drums he finds an electric oud, which descends from a family of string instruments used across the Middle East, North Africa, and Central Asia for thousands of years. Ahmed plugs it in and reels off a sizzling scale.

'In the seventies, we all wanted to be Jimmy Page,' he says with a grin.

Next, he unearths a tangled set of bagpipes, which he says were invented eons ago in Persia. When he gives them a blow, the noise is so loud my hands fly to my ears.

We move to the back corner of the studio where Ahmed clears away space in front of his computer. As I sit, with a few clicks of the mouse he pulls up recordings of Bahraini fidjeri performances. In the first video, a circle of men holding drums and clay pots sit in a room surrounded by milling onlookers. Their song starts softly, with hands thumping pots and slapping drums, and a lone singer carrying the melody. Then, there is a droning swell of voices as the rest of the men join in, lifting the original singer like a boat on the rising tide.

Fidjeri are the songs of the pearl divers. Historically, pearl divers were men from Africa, India, Sri Lanka, and the Gulf. Today, the pearl-diving industry in Bahrain has dwindled to a fraction of what it once was, and the divers are typically men from Bangladesh and the Philippines. The traditional songs of the pearl divers, though, drawn from the swirling churn of cultural influences that made up the pearl diver population, are still sung and celebrated widely. Created to be sung by those with lungs made powerful by diving, they speak of the long months at sea in the punishing summer heat, the dangers and the hardship, the hope and the fear. The melodies are chimerical, haunting, and strange.

In Bahraini lore, the origin of these pearl-diving songs is often credited to the supernatural. In these tales, the songs came into the knowledge of humanity on a summer night, long ago, when three friends were walking home. After spending an evening at the local tea house, the three friends were winding through the dark alleyways of the souq, as a sliver of moon watched overhead. Slowly, over the muffled noise of their footsteps, they began to notice a distant sound. What they heard, rolling into town off the warm wind coming from the coast, were the faint traces of a song. Voices, lilting notes, an enchanting rhythm. Looking at one another, in silent agreement the three friends turned to follow the uncanny melody.

The song pulled the men through the sleeping streets, past their homes and the places they knew, then past the edge of the souq, then beyond, to the shoreline itself. They hurried quickly through the soft sand, every moment growing more eager to reach the source of this strange tune. Waves lapping the shore to their right, the slumbering town to their left, the men walked faster, and then began to run.

Finally, they reached a small palm grove perched at the very edge of the sea. None of the men could be sure they had ever seen this grove before, if it was real or a dream. Slowing, they crept through the shadows that hung beneath the palm trees, moving toward the center of the grove; the smell of dark earth and ripening dates was rich in the air.

At the center of the grove, they found a white coral-stone building, radiant in the faint moonlight. Without having to speak, the friends knew they each thought that the building looked like nothing so much as a fine pearl, luminescent and pale as milk. From inside this building came the song.

Slowly approaching the open door, peering inside, the friends saw three shadowy, singing figures. As their eyes adjusted to the darkness of the building's interior, they noticed something striking about the singers: while they had the torsos of men, their legs were not the legs of human beings, but the legs of goats. As the singers swayed and sang their oceanic melody, their sharp black hooves rang out on the hard floor, lending an uncanny syncopation to the tidal melody. The singers were djinn.

When the djinn finished their song they turned to the men and, in unison, spoke. They said if the men would promise not to speak the name of God, they would teach them their songs. The men agreed to this demand and spent the night with the djinn learning their melodies, emerging from the palm grove at daybreak as if from a dream. In their hearts they now carried the song of the fidjeri to share, songs for every eventuality a pearl diver may face – songs for when the sea is rough, when the oyster beds cannot be found, when the boat heads out, when the boat heads in, when the divers are sick and hungry and feel forsaken.

The men singing from Ahmed's computer shift the song. It becomes more upbeat, raucous, and the drone of the melody feels stretched thin, as if something is about to break. As the song swells to its crescendo, from over my shoulder Ahmed

93

joins in. He effortlessly picks out a harmony with the singers and reels off the closing line.

31. Khobar, Saudi Arabia, 2021

At my feet, a silver puddle holds a slick of grease and the sheer light of dawn: red on purple on pink. Ripples. Early clouds, early wind, early heat. The air tastes of salt. The air tastes of my own air behind the surgical mask on my face. The air lifts the hair at the nape of my neck and I shiver.

Shopkeepers make their way down the street, sandals slapping at the dusty pavement. I watch them roll up the metal grating that locks down their shops at night. There are coronavirus pandemic signs on many of the windows, reminding passersby that masks are required, and there are scuffed social-distancing stickers on the sidewalks out front. There are also cats with weeping eyes peering out of alleys, pigeons rustling in rafters overhead, and a wheezing diesel truck rolling through the intersection behind me.

Walking down an alley, I emerge to find a breach of desert in the midst of the city, a block-long eruption of goldenweed, camphorweed, and spiny hopsage that is earlobe pink and earlobe soft and fluted upward as if listening to the long, singular voice of the sky. There is no sky like the Saudi sky, which is sky on sky on sky.

I weave through the shaggy grabbing plants, yanking the hem of my abaya off thorns and dusty leaves, until I find concrete, until I find asphalt, until I find where the sand once again yields to the city. Here, there is a shop whose side wall is taken up by a faded clothing advertisement. The faces of the models in the advertisement have been digitally rendered into indistinct blurs of pixelated flesh tones. This is not such a common sight as it used to be. Pixelated faces, along with mannequins whose faces have been carved away, while no longer common, do still linger in certain corners of the city, leaning out of their shops, telling their own Styrofoam stories from their anchorless gaze of the crowd.

Beyond this block that conjoins the brief desert breach, there are the remnants of Shula Mall, the mall of my childhood, a dim, airless place that both frightened and intrigued me. I remember its shops selling electronics, fresh juice, bootleg movies, and abayas and thobes and Fido Dido paraphernalia. There was a sign put up by a grocery store on the bottom floor that announced: *East is east and west is west but Shula is best!* Shula Mall burned down sometime in the mid-nineties – the exact year seems to change depending on who I ask, the memory of it somehow both searing and insubstantial.

I find a street of watch shops where there are timepieces on glittering display in every window. I stop at one on the corner of two empty streets, where tall shops and apartment blocks hem me in in every direction. When I lean closer to look at the merchandise in the window, I find a curious thing: none of the watches are showing precisely the same time. The variation isn't vast, a minute here, two minutes there, but I still feel as if I stumbled across a portal of some kind. I spend a long time standing in front of that window wondering what to do.

From here, if I go right, it is further into the souq, the souq of my childhood, the alleys where I can walk and remember the city that was, the self that was, the stories that were told, the stories that I am still waiting to tell. And if I go left from here, it is toward glitzy shopping malls and car dealerships and gourmet chocolate shops. I take one last look at the watches and then I turn left and proceed toward a part of the city that sometimes still feels new to me, though I have seen it grow from what it was to what it is today.

Some say there are certain parts of this city, the souq, for instance, that are more 'authentic' than others, but this is not strictly true. There was, after all, a time when the old souq itself, with its concrete pillars and air-conditioned shops, was new-fangled. When it comes to any city, authenticity is often largely a marketing concept, a way to bump up prices and ensnare gullible tourists. The emblems of modernity, like shopping malls, superhighways, and neon-lit chain restaurants, are as authentically Saudi, as legitimately Khaleeji, as the souqs, the date farms, or the dhow workshops. Too many stories written by outsiders about the Gulf still make a performance of marveling at its glossy shopping malls, as if they are more out of place here than they are anywhere else, as if there is any landscape where these behemoths are truly native.

The Eastern Province has, for millennia, been connected to trade networks that linked the people of the Arabian Gulf and Indian Ocean to Europe and East Asia. Being connected to these networks gave coastal reaches of the region a cosmopolitan feel; in addition to the local population, there were Indians, Baluchis, Afghanis, East Africans, Ottomans, and Persians. A city, like a self, is always pierced by currents of influence, innumerable ways of being and doing. My city, the city of these desert breaches, faceless faces, the burned-down husks of childhood malls, is authentic only to me. Authenticity is inherently relational, a reciprocal beholding of the other, a recognition that says, yes, this is indeed how it was between us and only us. The city that is authentic to me, after all, is not the city that is authentic to my parents, or to my grandparents, or to the woman I know who was born here nearly one hundred years ago, before there was readily available electricity, running water, or paved roads.

This woman has told me stories of her childhood, of the sweltering summer nights when her family would sleep on the roof of their house hoping to catch any hint of breeze, only to wake in the morning so thoroughly soaked by humidity that in the first groggy moments of consciousness she wondered if someone had tossed a bucket of water onto her. She tells a story of the first American she ever saw, a man who was wearing a suit and carrying a briefcase, and a story of her first ride in an automobile to a nearby oasis – a ride that she said marked the moment when everything began to change, a moment when she knew the future was coming fast.

This moment came to nearly every culture at some point, in every corner of the world, when so-called modernity forever altered the fabric of what was and replaced it with something that felt strange and fast. My great-grandmother, born in 1900, also pinned the moment everything changed to the arrival of the automobile. One day, when she was a young girl, she was picking cotton in a South Texas field when she heard a terrible roar in the distance. Never before had she heard a sound like this and she had no idea what it could be, but it kept on getting louder and louder, and closer and closer. Scared, she flung herself into a ditch beside the dirt road to hide from whatever the onrushing monstrosity was. Once the noise had reached its crescendo and passed, she chanced a look up to see what it was – and saw the first car she had ever seen. By the time, half a century later, my great-grandmother saw a man walk on the moon, she said nothing would surprise her anymore; anything that could happen would happen – and fast.

And for Saudi Arabia the future did come fast. In the 1930s, Khamis bin Rimthan, a Bedouin man from the ad-Dahna desert who was a noted expert in desert navigation, guided American geologist Max Steineke through the deserts of Arabia to map the land – and discover what lay underneath. The first six spots they discovered, when drilled, yielded disappointing results. But then, on March 4, 1938, from Rimthan and Steineke's seventh discovery – Dammam No. 7 – oil flowed at an astonishing rate.

While the conceptions of the pre-oil Gulf as a static land bereft of cultural confluence are mistaken, it is undeniable that the discovery of oil intensified cultural exchange. It was a reverberating moment that demarcated the past from the present, bringing stories of textural friction to the city streets, streets that filled, with dizzying speed, with new architecture, new products, new cultures, new languages, and new people.

One of the new people was my grandfather who moved to Saudi Arabia in 1957. An avid hobby photographer, he left us with a treasure trove of his photographs, taken from the time he arrived to the time he retired and left the Kingdom for good, more than thirty years later. In his early photos, I read a tension of witnessing. In one, a trio of American women, curls tightly coiffed around their smiling faces, shirt-waister dresses catching in the wind, gaze at a group of Saudi women in abayas who gaze back. My grandfather may have been living in Saudi Arabia, but in those early years his perspective still remained in America. In these photographs I think I can see that he viewed the land as something to be caught on film and shown to people elsewhere, people in distant countries who could not imagine these sun-blown streets. The landscape was a spectacle, a distant dream that he just happened to find himself inhabiting.

But, as the years and then the decades go by, the perspective captured by his photographs drifts as the stories he tells through his lens change. The Kingdom is no longer a strange new world, it has simply become home. In these later photographs, there is an intimacy of perspective, a noticing of meaning and whimsy. His eye is caught by the slanting fall of shadow from the neighborhood mosque minaret as it drapes itself across the pavement, and by a group of Saudi boys laughing uproariously with their hands spangled like stars around their faces, and by the curtain of moonlight falling through the leaves of a palm tree.

And, again and again and again, his eye is caught by the desert. From the window of a speeding car or standing still amid the dunes, in the first tinted light of dawn or in the day's last dregs of sun, again and again my grandfather took pictures of the desert. Though I never spoke to him about his photographs, never even knew the extent of his collection until after he died, I think I understand what he was trying to do. There is still, in these photographs of the desert, a tension of witnessing. But I am not sure it was only my grandfather doing the witnessing: something luminous beckons.

The company that originally had the concession to drill for oil in the deserts of Saudi Arabia was American with a globally diverse workforce, but in the 1970s the Kingdom negotiated the gradual purchase of company shares and, by 1980, increased its interest to one hundred percent. The long decades of cultural exchange fostered by the nascent oil industry, between Saudis and foreign workers, created bonds between individuals that are still celebrated today in the Kingdom's heritage museums. Many of the stories in these museums highlight how the initial wariness that may have characterized some of the early exchanges gave way to camaraderie, warmth, and lasting friendships. It was along these interpersonal frontiers that cultural understandings began to transform.

In the museum displays about these early pioneering days of the oil industry, the desert is always a central figure, often framed by the accoutrements needed to survive its ferocity. Behind glass on a weft of sand, there might be a dented canteen, a compass, a folded map. But, even here, when the desert is seen in an adversarial light, there is something of its majesty, something of the way it lingers on in the imaginations of the men who worked in its most remote reaches.

This ensnaring luminosity, photographed by my grandfather and recorded in the letters of the early oil workers, can also be found in the oral poetry of the Bedouin women of the Arabian Peninsula. Known as Nabati poetry, while popular, this oral poetry is often looked down upon by scholars because it is recited in dialectal Arabic, which is considered 'impure', and does not hew to the traditions considered 'proper' in classical poetry. Nabati poetry created by women in particular, as Moneera Al-Ghadeer writes, has long been overlooked in both Arabic and Western literary studies.[40] In *Desert Voices*, Al-Ghadeer seeks to redress this occlusion by examining women's oral poetry recorded in Abd Allah Ibn Raddas's *Shairat min Al-Badiyah*. Traveling through the Arabian Desert in the 1950s and 1960s, Ibn Raddas recorded oral poetry from Bedouin women in various regions of Saudi Arabia. His efforts not only preserved exquisite poetry but also provided a unique snapshot of Saudi Arabia at a time of significant change.

During these years, oil profits were transforming the Kingdom – new hospitals, schools, airports, and highways were being built at a rapid pace, infrastructure allowing running water and electricity to come to homes was put in place, and there was a marked increase in urbanization.[41] For Bedouins, whose goat hair tents were known as 'houses of poetry', this was a period when the stories they told about themselves were changing. Within the Gulf, Bedouins are the people traditionally associated with a nomadic lifestyle that revolves around the herding of livestock. There are differences, culturally, linguistically, and sartorially, between Bedouins and the settled populations, although, as Donald Cole contends, contrary to popular misconceptions, the divisions between the nomadic people and the settled people are not impermeable barriers but sites of diffusion rich with exchange.[42] Cole suggests that during the last century, the understanding of who a Bedouin was began to shift, as the term Bedouin – which used to describe people whose lifestyles centered on the herding of animals – began to connote an emblem of cultural identity that informs Khaleeji heritage narratives.

As Al-Ghadeer makes clear, in the poems recorded by Ibn Raddas the desert is more than a landscape, it is a repository of longing, a mode of thinking, and a cosmos of freedom. And, unlike foreign writers who tend to romanticize the Gulf's pre-oil past, these poets do not look at modern things like the automobile as foreign incursions inherently threatening to the desert itself or to their way of life. Rather, the automobile recurs in these poems as something that is incorporated into Bedouin existence, pulling in the new of the changing world.[43] In these poems, too, Al-Ghadeer highlights that the self and the self's multiplicity of emotion often fragment to pour through disparate focal points, both animate and not – as in the untitled poem by Bakhut Al Mariyah, in which her longing is both a she-camel grieving for her slaughtered calf and the drone of a Mack truck as it climbs a steep hill.

In these poems, the seamless slippage of narrative viewpoint between that which is the self and that which is *also* the self speaks to an understanding of inherent porosity. Here, the desert is both a landscape and a sophisticated metaphysical proposition that both encompasses and expands, rendering arbitrary delimitations obsolete. In this, these poems do not portray modernity as something inherently opposed to the natural. There are, in fact, not even clear distinctions between these two realms, as they bleed into one another with automobiles moving as nimbly through the desert as foxes or camels. In this they reflect an approach that does not recognize a firm dividing line between the so-called modern and premodern eras, nor automatically view them as in opposition.[44]

I am used to living inside a landscape of stories that appear to be in contention with one another, but, when I study these poems of the desert, I sense a radiance of space and a roving awareness that makes clear that an array of stories is not just possible, but is, in fact, the only way to approach what we may think of as truth. I linger in these poems, drinking in the agile way the narratorial mind drifts from a lonely lover to a circling hawk to the roaring engine of a Mack truck, and I try to see with the same spacious eye. To know that the onrushing future occupies the same space as the lingering past, that they are both able to be contained by the contiguous memory of the landscape, makes me begin to understand what Al-Ghadeer means when she writes that 'the desert is another name for love'.[45]

32.

Two years have passed and still I tell no one. I am suspicious of the concrete rigidity of the diagnosis; I don't have faith it will hold. The diagnostic borders of autism have expanded over the years to encompass more and more people, and sometimes I wonder if I want to be encompassed, if I want to be defined. As I have heard other autistic people ponder, if the borders of where I have been diagnostically placed shifted so dramatically in such a short time, who is to say what it will be like a few decades from now, will this diagnosis even still exist?

The psychiatric industry has a long history of 'diagnostic bracket creep'. This is when the profit-driven search for consumers for a new pharmaceutical product is the motivating factor behind more expansive diagnostic criteria; if more people are told their traits are pathological and fit under the rubric of a particular disorder, then there are more people who can be sold whatever pharmaceutical product has been created to treat said disorder. In recent years there has been an increasing awareness of psychiatric diagnoses among the general public, which has seen an increasing push from people themselves to be diagnosed. Svend Brinkmann suggests that, in this, diagnoses are no longer strictly medical concepts but ways in which people find meaning and make sense of their suffering.[46] Where in the past we may have framed our struggles in, for example, moral or spiritual terms, we now often view them solely as biologically rooted medical maladies. This is not to minimize the immense suffering that can arise from untreated mental illness, or to deny that there are innumerable people alive and thriving today because they sought psychiatric care. But, when we learn to view every one of our challenges with mental health as arising from a purely internal source, we may not consider the many other factors that can contribute to our well-being, or lack thereof. At a time when an increasing number of us live atomized lives – in which we are no longer deeply linked to family or religious belief or community or landscape ꟾ when we are given one of the last sanctioned avenues by which to define ourselves – the medicalization of our own experience – we cling to it.

As Majia Holmer Nadesan suggests, while there have doubtless been autistic people throughout history, it was not until the twentieth century, with its focus on childhood development and psychology, that autism was formalized as a discrete clinical diagnosis.[47] Nadesan argues that our understanding of what autism is, and who it is that should fall within its borders, is socially constructed through the stories we tell – not only about autism but also about what kind of behavior is 'normal' and what kind of behavior is not. Understanding the socially constructed aspects of autism as a diagnosis, she says, does not deny any possible biological factors, but allows us to consider the ways in which our understanding of autism is socially produced.

I know there are those who believe we should eschew any kind of label, and there is a part of me – a roving, mercurial part – that instinctively bristles at anything too definitive. But having the story of autism as a lens through which to understand my life has felt revelatory. Knowing that I am autistic, in our current understanding of what that term means, anyway, has given me permission to stop believing the stories I was always told about myself – that I am lazy and uptight, that I am fundamentally wrong in some way. When I couldn't do the things I saw so many other people doing with seeming ease, I had always assumed that I was at fault, that there was some inherent failing within me that meant I so often felt miserable in situations that others could tolerate or even enjoy. There is, it turns out, not an endless series of failures and a mysterious inability to function properly; there is something that ties it all together and strings a cohesive narrative from what previously looked like disparate parts. This doesn't mean that I am freed from all responsibilities or

103

from striving to make the most of my life, but it does mean that with this diagnosis, with this label, my life has a story that makes sense.

But I do wish that the wider conception of autism was not so thoroughly rooted in a pathological understanding of the natural diversity of the human mind. The diagnosis, after all, is autism spectrum *disorder*. This approach to cognitive diversity, in which divergences are always considered wholly problematic, is known as the 'pathology paradigm'. It teaches that there are ways that the human mind operates that are typical and therefore normal and therefore good, and then there are ways the human mind operates that are atypical and therefore abnormal and therefore bad. In this paradigm, autism is sometimes seen as something extraneous to the 'real' person, something that is hiding the supposedly true self. It is clear, then, why so many experts who see autism in this light picture it as something that needs to be cured or eradicated, with often devastating consequences for the autistic people who must suffer these interventions.

I admit that I can rarely live up to the neurotypical conventions expected by the world, but those conventions are arbitrary; they are not immutable laws of nature. Not being able to live up to them does not automatically make someone faulty, and yet that is the verdict decreed by medical science. After all, in the vast and wooly vicissitudes of human experience and behavior, there are no clear-cut borders between typical and atypical. As is commonly said in the autistic community, autistic traits are first and foremost human traits, which means they can be experienced and expressed by anyone in various ways. What makes someone possibly diagnosable, within the current medical approach, is if they show these traits to such a degree that it has a significant impact on their ability to function in a so-called 'normal' way. But, again, here are more stories to unravel. Normal? What does that mean? Is it the best story we have to make sense of the wild vagaries of human behavior?

There are other stories, stories that do not automatically pathologize all variations in human neurocognition, that do not see autism as a series of checklist behaviors collated by non-autistic doctors or view it as a tragic disorder that must be eradicated at all costs. One of these stories is found within the neurodiversity paradigm. Nick Walker suggests that the term 'neurodiversity' refers to the natural diversity found within human minds across our species. Just as we expect to find diversity across the human population in regard to other characteristics, we should also expect to find diversity within neurocognitive functioning. From this understanding emerged the neurodiversity paradigm, which recognizes our collective neurodiversity as not only natural but a strength that is beneficial for humanity.[48] The term 'neurodivergent', coined by Kassiane Asasumasu, means having a mind that functions in a way deemed by society to be atypical. This includes autism, ADHD, OCD, Tourette's, and much more. The neurodiversity paradigm does not deny that there are forms of neurodivergence, such as traumatic brain injuries, that people may desire to be cured of, but it does preclude the notion of there being such a thing as a hypothetically 'normal' brain from which neurodivergent people diverge. Rather, as Walker suggests, it is the constellation of behaviors that society has deemed normal from which they diverge. The difference may seem subtle but its significance is profound.

Human behavior, the self itself, our ability to function, all of these can fluctuate significantly and in these fluctuations we can drift closer or further from what our society deems normal at any given time. In much the same way that it can be illuminating to recognize the transcultural influences that make up our own personal cultural identity, and in so doing be more accepting of those we may have formerly thought of as 'other', it can likewise also be illuminating to recognize all the many ways we ourselves diverge from what our society deems normal and therefore 'neurotypical'. The more that we do this, the more we can approach 'neuro-cosmopolitanism', the ability of a person – or a community – to welcome and live easily with people with every variation of neurology, moving beyond mere tolerance to an enthusiastic embrace of neurodivergence.[49]

I am grateful to have been identified as autistic, and it is my hope that everyone who needs and wants it will be able to access the same service. A correct diagnosis is not accessible to everyone. Two people with identical behavioral traits can be diagnosed with different conditions based on their sex, age, ethnicity, class, or any number of variables, any of which can be exacerbated by a doctor's prejudices or lack of knowledge. Some doctors still operate on diagnostic criteria that is woefully out of date, with no understanding of masking, and refuse to consider autism in people who, for example, can make eye contact or are happily married. Those autistic people who are overlooked are then denied accommodations and information they have a right to, not least of which is the self-knowledge diagnosis brings. This self-knowledge can be, literally, lifesaving.

There are those who say that neurodivergent people should not in any way celebrate being neurodivergent, that we should either speak only about the difficulties we face or just shut up altogether and struggle on in supposedly quiet dignity, lest we give the impression that our lives are anything but unrelenting misery. Apparently, if we find anything positive to say about the way our minds work, we are glamorizing disability in a purportedly dangerous way. This toxic message attempts to dictate the way our stories should unfold. This thinking says that when we tell our stories – *if*, that is, we are even allowed to – we have to do it in the way that non-autistic people want. In this way, we are absented from our own narratives and told the only story we should tell is one of hardship. As Martin Shaw suggests, it seems that many people today have fallen into a strange reverie, believing that if we only dig around in our wounds long enough the pain alone will suffice for meaning.[50] But pain is only a signpost on the road toward potential meaning; it is not a worthy endpoint in itself. When we confuse the two we stay mired in isolation; it is only when we look up that we realize that the landscape unfurls around us in all directions.

The way I perceive and relate to being autistic is not inherently 'right' or shared by all autistic people, and I wouldn't claim to speak on behalf of anyone else. All autistic people, like all non-autistic people, are different, so the story I tell is only *my* story – and only one of my stories at that. The way I feel about this, as with so much else, is contrary and contradictory, mercurial and manifold. In a world that increasingly expects easy-to-digest sound bites of self, I want to slip liquid and fast, to preserve the potential that resides in the chthonic primordial form. This does not make me nothing, it makes me, potentially, anything.

33. Muharraq, Bahrain, 2022

This island is an island that tilts toward the strange and this summer there are, everywhere, outcroppings of weird. Unchaperoned on the corner between a cold store and a school, there is a group of mannequins, plastic skin blazing opalescent in the noonday sun. At the end of the street is a painting an artist has left on a stretch of empty wall – it is of a half-open door; ferns and flowers billow out, so realistically lush that I almost believe I could push the door open and reveal a hidden garden.

This summer, Muharraq is in a state of surreal serendipity. Cohesion between various neighborhoods is whimsical and imprecise. Echoes are replete, the walls of buildings drip with them. My ears capture the manifold renditions of bird wings, laughter, the backfiring of car engines, and the sharp clatter of donkey hooves on hot asphalt. I cross thresholds and stand on corners and linger in empty courtyards. Everywhere, there is the sense of space opening up in the city, space where something used to be, space that can now be filled with wonder.

Through this space I walk and I revel and I speak. Words pour from my tongue in a great shimmering stream – fundug, coagulate, habhab, siphon, sepulchral – clots of verbs and rushing tributaries of nouns, English and Arabic together. This is not speaking in the traditional sense, this is making a spectacle of speech – the real has been replaced by the representation, which digs up even deeper meaning – and I mimic and thrill and explode.

language + meanings across cultures - Could another language better describe what I want to say?

As a child, once I had the trick of speech it did not slow for years. At the time, I didn't know how to explain how necessary it was, that if the words did not get on the outside of me they would detonate on the inside. It felt to me as if my brain was one of those open-mouthed whales we learned about in school, but instead of gobbling down krill, it swept up thousands upon thousands of units of information. The input was ceaseless, rich, textured, varied, urgent, with each particle conjuring a host of resonant associations that in turn had their own associations, each with its own ability to coax emotion and memory and sensorial response. Just being in the world felt like being on the verge of falling into a mental whirlpool of information. Words, then, this constant speech, was my attempt to equalize some of that input. - Writing

The words that came most naturally to me as a child, and still now, were often ornate and multi-syllabic. They were unusual enough to raise eyebrows. Quickly, I learned to veer away from the first word my mind offered up, whether it was one of my own making or one of the gilded, majestic words I rapturously hoarded, to search for a simpler substitution that would be less likely to make others smirk or roll their eyes. Perhaps, as other late-diagnosed autistics, like Katherine May, have suggested, the 'communication difficulty' often included in standard autistic diagnostic criteria does not always refer to a lack of words or the struggle to conjure speech, but rather the difficulty that arises when there is a surplus of words, words that, in hyperlexic children like myself, are often considered too advanced or complex, too strikingly unusual to be used in everyday speech.[51]

There was nothing apparently linear about my abundant speech, either. For many years I didn't understand that was even required. What I did know was that others could not keep up with my jagged, darting thought process. A childhood friend said I moved from topic A to topic Z with only three or four steps in the middle. She called it 'random firing' and would ask me to explain the trail of connections that I insisted were there. This was my first understanding that not everyone saw everything as being connected, and that the way my thoughts ordered themselves (disparate, flashes of lightning, waterfalls of constant motion) was not universal. I did not, at the time, know the term 'orthogonal thinking', or that it is increasingly considered a hallmark of autistic thought. To the outside observer, it may look like there are no connections between the individual thoughts, so distant are the topics, but to the autistic thinker the connection is radiantly obvious. The connection, often long trails of connection, can feel like a strobe light of images, of words, even consonants or etymological similarities, of memories, of sensory impressions, but the connections are there and they are replete with meaning. What this feels like, in practice, is a mind that spins so fast the whole world threatens to come apart at the seams. For autistic people, this type of associative thinking – forming connections between seemingly unrelated subjects – can come effortlessly. As Ralph James Savarese observes, when autistic children grow up, unlike many of their neurotypical counterparts, they retain an animistic conception of the world as profoundly interrelated and radiantly alive.[52]

This summer in Muharraq is a travesty of connection. My head spins with it. I am in too many places at once, moving through alleys with the pearl merchants of centuries past, sitting in tea shops filled with the image of Umm Kulthum a thousand times over, in secret gardens of green surrounded by strangers watching gulls drift across the sky. There is, for each of us, a different city: for instance, this city is my only city and to it I will never belong. There is this moment and the shockwave of nothing else: *here I am here I am here I am.*

34. Karanah, Bahrain, 2018

Ancient pots filled with snake skeletons and pearls: calcified and gleaming and fragile and real. Four thousand years old, lined up behind glass beneath a spotlight. When I lean forward they are a thousand bright moons caught in self-contained nights of darkest clay. It is a benevolence, this archaic dispensation from time itself, that they have survived this long so that they can now line a shelf in a museum where I roam.

Everything smells of salt and low-tide and through the tall windows I hear the yips of wild dogs. Also, through the great glass windows, I cannot see the horizon because an old crumbling fort takes its place. Along the Gulf's coastlines, forts sprang up to guard oases, harbors, and pearl banks, towering, sedentary sentinels that stood in stark contrast to the nomadic tribes of the desert interior. These forts were bastions of inert splendor, imposing piles of mud, brick, and plaster. The site on which this particular fort was built was continually inhabited for thousands of years by a succession of different civilizations, as well as home to outcroppings of Kassites, Persians, and Greeks. It was also here, in the 1950s, that the legendary Dilmun civilization came back to life.

For years Dilmun was believed to be nothing more than a myth spun by Sumerian bards, a fantastical land where beasts did not kill and where men did not grow old. Then, an English archeologist, Geoffrey Bibby, began work in Bahrain, and he and his team discovered evidence that thousands of years ago there actually had been a Dilmun civilization. It had been vast and powerful, stretching tendrils throughout the Gulf. Suddenly, what was once lost, was very real.

To ancients, Dilmun's famed pearls were known as the 'Flower of Immortality' and Dilmun itself was the 'Land of the Living'. In *The Epic of Gilgamesh*, Dilmun is where Gilgamesh journeys in search of immortality. His friend Enkidu – his partner in a myriad of violent revels and daring feats – has died and Gilgamesh, wracked with grief, is preoccupied with the notion of his own eventual death. It consumes his thoughts and his dreams, stalking him on his voyage. By the time he finds his way to Dilmun and meets Utnapishtim, a survivor of a cataclysmic flood granted immortality by the gods, Gilgamesh is willing to do anything to attain everlasting life.

He recounts his tale of grief to Utnapishtim and admits that when Enkidu died he, Gilgamesh, became aware of his own mortality, and for the first time knew what it was to fear death. In response, Utnapishtim tells him that to die is the fate of all men and Gilgamesh must accept his destiny. Hearing this, Gilgamesh is distraught. Eventually, giving in to the urging of his wife, Utnapishtim reveals to Gilgamesh a divine secret: at the bottom of the sea there lies a plant that will restore him to his youth (believed to refer to pearl-bearing oysters). Elated, Gilgamesh binds stones to his feet and dives beneath the waves, resurfacing with the plant. He decides to return to his kingdom and test it on an old man to see if it really works. But, before he can, the plant is stolen away by a snake.

When I read this tale I cannot help but wonder if Gilgamesh's search for a way to live forever was not only about evading death, but also about never being forgotten. The fear of death is not just the fear of the unknown, after all, but ultimately the fear of *being* unknown. We know that we die, and we spend our lives trying to make sense of that. We tell ourselves who we are, reifying our identity to others and to ourselves so that we are known in a myriad of ways; this nation, not that; this belief, not that; this diagnosis, not that. As Arianna Dagnino writes:

> [We] invent fictions of our selves (as nations do with cultures) to offer to others and to ourselves coherent and structured narratives of our lives, while in fact we are but the result of uncontrolled and involuntary series of constant transformations, complexities, contradictions, and paradoxes.[53]

The Epic of Gilgamesh is a legendary drift concerning the oldest fear of all. This ancient fear was well known to the Dilmuns who recreated in their ritual pots the crux of their beliefs about life and death: the pearl – the 'plant' that restores youth – and the snake, who stole it away. Pot after pot, row after row, snake after snake, coiled around nuclei of pearl, delicately assembled and reverently buried thousands of years ago by the hands of people long dead, subjects of an empire that was forgotten for longer than it existed.

35. Budaiya, Bahrain, 2019

We sit in the red evening cracking pistachios and swapping words for love. My friend says she feeds eleven cats every night, with the leavings of chicken carcasses and buttered rice, and I can see feline eyes even now glowing in the shadows of the garden shrubbery like glinting, blinking flowers. When prayer call begins they emerge, pink tongues darting between teeth. She tells me the cats' names, but I can't remember any of them except the one: Susan. My friend heard the name on a sitcom once and loved it so much she says she always makes sure to name one of her cats Susan. When the Susans die there is always another Susan come to take their place. Sometimes, the

Susans are boys, but it doesn't matter, she explains, because an English name is just a pleasant sound bereft of meaning.

Her villa is one of the oldest in the neighborhood and it wants to be a story unto itself. Open-air courtyards make a cathedral of the sky and bright lamps jewel every corner. She tells me she has spent two decades making this house a home and now she will never leave. She says they will have to carry her out of the front door in a shroud.

She asks me if I want hibiscus tea. Her jalabiya is bright green and her house slippers are yellow and she moves slowly because her hips ache. Not arthritis, though, she says. A car accident that should have killed her but didn't. She shakes her head, remembering, and then she shuffles into her kitchen, calling for the maid. While she is gone I watch the cats watching me and I tell them hello.

One of them, Susan perhaps, rubs its pink nose against my ankle. When my friend returns she mentions another word for love, old and passed over by most, but one that she knows because her mother, who came from a faraway land with an entire galaxy of tongues, taught her. She makes me repeat the syllables, reaching with her fingers to push at my cheeks to get the sound just right. She smells like black lemons and sugar.

36. Dhahran, Saudi Arabia, 2021

I walk in pursuit of the marvelous, in a spiraling, oneiric drift toward the weird. Sensing the fundamental warp beyond the plastic bustle of the crowd, I seek to point it out: ethereal, ecstatic, transcendent, look, look right here.

In the transcultural deviation from the norm there is subversion that offers useful distortions. We exist in a constant state of translation, not only linguistically, but culturally, which is a sort of language itself, a field in which one can be fluent, an assemblage of rules and meaning that one can navigate.

Transcultural people – or cross-cultural people or adult third-culture kids; whatever term you need to capture the weirdness of stuffing multiple cultures into a single individual – slip and dart orthogonally between the crevices to conjure connections where before there was only empty space, knowing that the most cherished things are never original, but outcroppings upon outcroppings upon outcroppings. Not even space is ours alone, not even our memories of a place are pure and uncontested.

Sometimes when I am walking I can feel bubbles of compressed time rising up from the current of the street, displacing intention, warping the pull of gravity with their weight. Because of this, there is never any equilibrium in the city, something is always tipping me one way or the other, into the future, or back into a past.

37. Dammam – Riyadh – Ta'if
Jeddah, Saudi Arabia, 1965

There is the soft and bony press of strangers' bodies, Umm Kulthum too loud on the radio, and the desert wind coming through the open window, whipping and wild. My thirteen-year-old father, Rodney, and his two young friends are rocketing down a ribbon of highway spooled through the desert, heading to Riyadh. They are on their own, with no adult supervision, and the feeling of freedom is intoxicating.

Between them, the passengers in the shared taxi pass parcels of roasted pumpkin seeds and salted pistachios. The sharp crack of shells between teeth is the only sound to pierce the roar of music. Hours pass when no one speaks, everyone staring out at the unchanging desert, their eyes slowly sharpening, picking out fine details and granular specifics until finally the desert is anything but changeless and is made fresh with every look.

Full darkness falls and the taxi slows and bumps off the road, stopping in front of a small cinderblock building topped with a corrugated tin roof. A few trucks are scattered around and there is a shed to one side with spare tires and canisters of oil and gasoline. The passengers spill out, stretching legs and arms, heading for the hammam, pulling out cigarettes, and clearing their throats into the dry soil. An older man clambers out of the back seat. Heavy set, with thickets of eyebrows over pale eyes, he tells the boys he needs a drink and begins looking around for a hose.

While everyone else gathers at the large clay pot near the doorway that contains sweet water, this man finds a hose, turns it on, holds it to his mouth and drinks his fill. Pausing to wipe his face, he shouts at the boys: 'Raw water has all the health benefits the body needs! Minerals! Vitamins!'

Inside the rest stop: stale air thick with cigarette smoke and the bitter scent of old cooking oil. Out-of-date automotive calendars line the pockmarked walls, and, in a corner shadowed with cobwebs, a single potted plant leans toward death. There are shelves along one wall that display an assortment of Chinese-made food stuffs, like tins of beans and dry biscuits.

A cook eyes the group from the kitchen while the waiter brings out bottles of warm soda. Orders are not taken but dinner is served quickly: thick discs of flat bread act as plates for rice and kabsa that is eaten between pinched fingers. After dinner there is strong tea and sweet dates and jarak smoked from a tall water-pipe, until everyone feels fizzy with caffeine and sugar and tobacco. The road beckons and the driver nods and heads for the car; they won't stop again until they reach the capital.

At midnight, the taxi drops the boys off at a squat hotel near the Riyadh city center. Inside, they find a receptionist dozing on a threadbare couch. When they wake him, he seems unsurprised to find them standing there, as if unaccompanied teenagers appear this time every evening asking for a room. Handing them a kerosene lantern, he points to a narrow set of stairs. At the top, the boys find a room with pink and green plaster walls and sleeping mats on the floor.

The boys drop their bags and move as one to the room's single window. Leaning out, they find the city slumbering all around them. From somewhere in the distance they can hear the ghostly howling of wild dogs. For Rodney, the moment is hushed and momentous. As he stares out at the strange geometry of the city he realizes this is the farthest he has ever been on his own from home.

Salat al fajr comes early. The sun will not rise for some time yet and the city outside is quiet, save for the muezzin calling worshippers to prayer from a nearby minaret with a crystalline voice – al-salaatu khayrun min al-nawn – prayer is better than sleep. The boys rise and head out to meet the day.

Their first stop is Qasr al-Masmak – Masmak Fort. The fort won't be made into a heritage museum for another thirty years and for now is used to store military equipment, so there are no other visitors, just the boys and the posted guards and the birds rustling in the palm trees. The whole space is quiet, as if the fort has absorbed the sounds around it, muffling them away to nothing.

In school, every year during Rodney's childhood, he and his classmates have been shown a film that features a dramatic reenactment of the night King Abdulaziz and his warriors retook Masmak Fort. Seeing it in person feels like stepping into a legend come to life.

After three days of footsore wandering and visiting old school friends, days of goat kabsa and nights of wild dog howling, the boys find another shared taxi and begin the journey to the western reaches of the Kingdom. Over many hours, the hard flat brightness of the Najd softens, giving way to swaybacked

116

hills and somber skies. They stop for the night at a roadside rest stop where they sleep on the dirt floor and have cold rice and warm soda for breakfast. On they travel, until the swaybacked hills give way to the mist-hung Al-Sarawat mountains of the Hejaz, where shaggy hillocks of juniper hug the winding roads and give off the smudgy scent of scalded lemon and cedar wood.

Entering the city of Ta'if, the taxi slows to pass a roadside stand selling figs and jars of honey that glow like tiny suns in the afternoon light. Known as the Garden of the Hejaz, Ta'if receives plentiful rainfall compared to the rest of the Kingdom – one of the most arid countries on Earth – which allows it to cultivate crops like wheat, coffee, and its famous flowers.

Rodney searches the crowd, eyes scanning the heads of the men for flashes of color and wisps of green. There! A young man at the side of the road is wearing a crown of marigolds and dense green basil, a halo wrought in flowers and leaves. Farther on are two men wearing garlands of rose and jasmine. These men are from the Qahtan tribe, who wear floral crowns both for their beautiful appearance and to ward off illness.

After the uniformly pale mud buildings of Riyadh, the boys are dazzled by the medley of color in Ta'if – buildings of dark stone with pale green, dusty blue, and soft yellow highlights all jumble next to one another. In the souq, unveiled women dressed in the colorful patterns of the Hejaz sell apricots, pomegranates, and dates, while men in blue thobes sell goat hair cloaks and stacks of firewood.

Making their way to the outskirts of town, the boys find themselves on a road flanked with juniper and scrubby brush. They smell the famed roses of Ta'if before they see them: man-sized mountains lining the dirt path, pyramids of frothy pink rose petals interspersed with smaller piles of orange marigolds, pale jasmine, and more besides, indigo and cerulean and inky burgundy, towers of color waiting to be crushed and boiled.

In the center of this field of color, there is a wooden shack. Out front, gleaming copper pots catch the shifting mountain light, casting off sunbursts and steaming clouds of fragrance. The cauldrons are filled with bushels of the pinkest rose petals gently simmering in water, while hanging overhead are complicated rigs of tubing that catch the steam and condense it until only the most potent oils remain. The Egyptian men manning the cauldrons laugh at the boys' delight and let them take turns at the long wooden paddles used to stir the mixtures.

This particular strain of rose was first brought to Saudi from the Balkans by the Ottomans, who controlled parts of the Hejaz for nearly 400 years between the sixteenth and twentieth centuries. To the surprise of the Ottomans, the roses that grew in Ta'if surpassed in both color and scent the ones they had cultivated elsewhere. The production of rose attar was originally done in Mecca, with sacks of petals ferried by camel out of the mountains and delivered to the Indian pharmacists of the holy city. But 200 years ago the craft was brought to Ta'if to make the process more efficient and to better preserve the rose's delicate oils. Ta'ifi rose attar quickly became beloved throughout the Muslim world; pilgrims visiting Mecca traditionally purchase a vial – called a tolah, an Indian unit of measurement – as a souvenir of their journey.

For the next several days the boys smell of rose. They eat rosewater muhalbiya al ruz, thumb rose attar behind their ears upon waking, drink rose-petal tea after every meal, and buy rose incense in the souq. They also listen to the whisper of the rain and watch the mist rise off the hunched backs of the mountains. They feel web-caught by the town's soft magic and imagine staying for weeks, for months. They want to see the hillsides change with the seasons and see the next crop of flowers bloom. But they must move on.

Driving to Jeddah in another shared taxi, the boys are cramped in the back seat and feel sour, tired, hungry. They have to detour around the holy city of Mecca, which only Muslims may enter, before turning once again for the Red

Sea coast. When they finally see Jeddah, rising like steam from the vivid blue of the sea, it is like nothing they had imagined. The buildings are the tallest they have seen yet, elaborate with latticework balconies, and the streets are full of cars and fashionable people and glass-fronted shops and advertisements and restaurants. It is almost Hajj and there are so many people from all over the world crowding these streets to make their pilgrimage to Mecca that the city hums with intensity.

The boys go first to the historic center of town, walking with their heads craned back staring up in wonder at the towering, centuries-old, coral-stone houses with hand-carved teak balconies, bright blue window shutters, and ornately carved doors. Then they are in the sleekly modern new section of town, where they find shops selling luxury goods from all over the world. They spend hours in spotless stores peeking at display cases of watches and high-end radios and even television sets, surrounded by the smell of furniture polish and expensive cigarettes. People stop them on the streets, curious to know where they are from, why they've come to Jeddah, and how much money their fathers make. The Arabic here is different than that of the Eastern Province and the boys, with their Sharqiyah accents, must work to be understood. Many of the people who stop them are Hajjis, keen to tell the boys that it is their first time in the Kingdom.

On their final day, the boys drift toward a souq that is spread out in an empty lot by the sea. The space of the souq opens suddenly, a billowing of the street, bright and crowded and full of color. There are Nigerian women with gele turbans wound around their heads, Somali women in their jilbabs, Egyptian men wearing blazer coats over pale dishdashas, Indonesians in white thobes and batik sarongs, and Yemenis with janbiya gleaming at their hip.

Rodney is familiar with the pilgrims who begin their journey on the other side of the Kingdom in the Eastern Province, those coming from India and Pakistan and Bangladesh and

Iran. Those pilgrims pass through his town on their way to Mecca, bringing with them goods from home to sell all across the country to fund their pilgrimage journey – Persian carpets, Baluchi rugs, or Indian furniture – seeding their cultural touchstones throughout the land. But never before has he seen the pilgrims who arrive on the Kingdom's western shores: the Eritreans, Moroccans, Libyans, and Kenyans.

Each group has claimed their own area of the souq, tossed out large rugs, and spread their wares. There are dried nuts, bolts of colorful cloth, shawls and scarves, hand-tooled sandals, bundles of cinnamon and herbs, dishes of pearls and semi-precious stones, jars of pungent oud, and ivory-handled knives. There are people selling and buying, people eating and drinking, people resting, and people shouting.

Leaving his friends behind, Rodney ricochets through the multitude, letting himself be buffeted by the crowd, turning and turning again until he is floating in the currents of motion and color, buoyed by sound and scent. He will be leaving Jeddah in just a few hours, catching a shared taxi all the way across the Kingdom heading for home. His journey is over but this moment, lit by the wild salt scent of the Red Sea, and dense with the roar of the souq crowd, feels like it could last forever.

38.

Maybe to be autistic is to be from the interstices, and to there-fore be transcultural, in a most fundamental way. Aspects of the embodied autistic experience, suggests Ralph James Savarese, mean that an autistic individual, by simply existing, can be a testament to alternative ways of being.[54] Perhaps, as Yergeau says, 'To be autistic is to live and to lie in a between space.'[55]

While the etymological roots of the word 'autism' refer to the belief that autistics are inordinately self-focused, Chris

Martin suggests it is often autistic people who are exceedingly perceptive of the surrounding world, a perception not limited to other humans, but open to connections with trees, rocks, animals, even weather patterns.[56] Contrary to persistent stereotypes that say autistic people cannot feel compassion for others, a common conversation among autistic people is how we are so often overwhelmed by compassion and empathy, so much so that it can make it difficult to function, to explain, to even leave the house because it is inevitable you will see horrors in the world – like the pigeons dead on the road, their soft grey feathers, discolored by the wheels of the cars who drive over them, ruffling in the wind, and you know this will make a pain in your throat like a clenched fist so that you cannot breathe and cannot speak and cannot think. This kind of empathy is transfiguring; it makes you into an other.

The autistic penchant for flowing beyond the conventional bounds of perception is reflected in the unique ways in which autistic people use language. Julia Miele Rodas notes:

> From the beginning, it has been widely agreed that autistic people use language in unusual ways. From mutism to metaphor, from abstraction to repetition, syntax, word choice, logorrhea, monologuing, echolalia, inversion, precision, neologism, and formulaic use of words, autistic language is startling, inventive, challenging, irregular.[57]

In Julie Brown's observation of the unique literary and creative characteristics found in classic authors whom she believes may have been autistic, she notes that these writers often use a collage-like process for assembling their drafts, perhaps influenced by the autistic proclivity for fragmentation, and that their tendency to extensively quote from other authors in their writing is connected to autistic echolalia.[58] Noting that autistic writers often write autobiography, Brown suggests that they do so in ways that may not always be easily comprehendible to the typical reader. Suggesting that autistic individuals may feel somewhat reticent about definitively conveying the self through writing, Brown notes there may even be a tendency for these writers to rewrite their autobiography regularly, as did Hans Christian Andersen, perhaps reflecting an intuitive understanding of the unsettled reality of the self. Brown also observes that autistic writers are highly experimental even when working in established genres, partake in ostensible randomness, utilize repetition, are often hyperlexic and display a passion for volatile, exuberant language, and portray setting by focusing on a conglomeration of details, to such an extent that description dominates the text, becoming, in fact, more important than characters or even plot.

While autistic linguistic and creative traits have long been viewed as nothing more than signs of pathology, Rodas argues that these traits are suffused with meaning, that they are, in fact, exhilarating literary techniques with the power to 'disturb, disrupt, and undo'.[59] In this view, autism can be perceived as an aesthetic unto itself; in this way it is, in fact, an art.[60]

39.

Now, when I walk I walk knowing why I want to write the street the way I want to write the street. Now, when I spend an hour in a tiny corner shop – a baqala or cold store – gasping at the intensity of perfection I find within its colorfully disheveled shelves and vertiginous stacks of sundries, I give in to the autistic 'collecting impulse that attends the ephemeral . . . that which builds toward climax by means of repetition, obsessions, stiltedness, echo'[61] and I write a poem about the detergents and perfumes and boxes of Vimto and stacks of cigarettes and the silvery bags of crisps hanging from the ceiling like stalactites and Vimto Vimto Fizzy Vimto Fizzy Watermelon Remix

Chips Oman Beebee Battle chewing gum red tea cardamom apples covered in wax orca floatie giraffe floatie pony floatie Teletubby floatie jareesh sumac drumsticks cumin nonalcoholic beer mango chutney carrot chutney mango carrot hot chili achar chutney Eagle rulan cake Nestomalt high energy drink Thai Rose long-grain rice Bahar Dettol purple pickled garlic Fair & Lovely soap Virginity Restore soap purple cauliflower local calling card international calling card Nido powdered milk 100-year-old eggs red lentils yellow lentils rose halwa with pumpkin seeds and saffron jasmine perfume oud perfume Rani float Haleem mix Anchor powdered milk Partner kitchen scissors Primo soap Omo detergent Lux abaya wash Rulo Nut biryani mix curry mix tamarind dab sauce Choki stick karak tea haleeb tea red tea shalky shalky dress miswaq stick cut and uncut India Kings Insignia Inspiro Intro Turkish labneh Saudi labneh Cypriot halloumi Indian ghee Maggi juicy chicken za'atar meat masala Madras curry National mutton biryani Eastern rasam powder bitter gourd sweetcorn chow chow koosa snake gourd ash gourd tender coconut longan fruit India chickoo lychee fruit packet with syrup sweet tamarind with sugar physalis kaka fruit Lulu Pinoy sugar palm fruit Datu Puti native vinegar Lady's Choice sandwich spread Mother's Best banana ketchup Jufran hot banana sauce Bagoong barrio fiesta shrimp paste Doux frozen chicken 7 Days swiss roll Dac disinfectant Persil abaya shampoo Panda ear buds Private Clip night Private ultra Missteen Sunova hand soap Sadia chicken griller Rana tomato paste Nour sunflower oil Shams sunflower oil Sumdum mutton sambusa Anlene low fat cream powder Goody pineapple slices Garameesh rusk whole wheat Bugles corn snack Royal beef kebab Majdi laurel leaves Nahool mini raisin cake Al Safi long-life milk Deemah mamoul tea biscuit Americana hamburger with Arabic spices Americana frozen vegetables mix Mars Bar Chocola's Telephone Sella Muzza rice Pringles Pot Crisps original Pringles Pot Crisps hot and spicy Baity milk powder Brossard brownie chocolat et pépites

Al Kabeer Arabic kofta Galaxy Jewels Hershey's Syrup Victoria Garden hommos tahina Syrian eggplant Halwani Brothers halwa plain Marami potato chips Lambweston twister potatoes Baidar tomato ketchup Borgat jubnah crackers Al Shifa honey Al Joud macaroni Perfetto fischioni rigatti Gandour yamama Loacker wafer quadratini Foster Clark's baking powder Sunbullah kubee Coopoliva green pitted olives Freshly natural slice mushroom Kiri al jarra Teashop Taib cracker Majdi cardamom Danette Flan chocolate Nunu baby shampoo

40.

Picture the author as she types – she sways and as she sways she rubs her thumbnail against her lip and as she rubs her thumbnail against her lip she blinks and as she blinks she murmurs and as she murmurs she warbles and as she warbles she types:

Self-stimulation is an ungainly term used to describe a transcendent autistic practice. Self-stimulation, or stimming, as it is known in the autistic community, is a way of using the body to seek sensory stimulation to achieve a multitude of different aims. Stimming can include a vast array of behaviors, including rocking back and forth, swaying, flapping the hands, spinning, rubbing the fingers, gazing at flashing lights, smelling or sniffing, repeating specific words or phrases, twirling the hair, or touching a certain texture. The aims of stimming are varied and they differ from autist to autist and from situation to situation. Some of the sought outcomes include blocking out unpleasant stimuli, regulating the internal state, communicating a thought or expressing an emotion, integrating input, and maintaining concentration. Sometimes stimming is also about maintaining the feeling of being embodied; in stillness, it can feel as if the body vanishes, and so movement is required to summon it into existence once again. Stimming, then, can be a way to be a body.

We all stim, autistics and non-autistics alike. When you drum your fingers against the table during a dull meeting, or when you bounce your leg up and down when nervous, or when you idly twirl a lock of hair between your fingers while watching a movie, that is stimming. Autistics, though, take stimming to stunning creative heights, doing it with a verve and intensity rarely seen in non-autistics.

Like so many other autistic traits and behaviors, stimming has long been seen by many parents, teachers, and therapists as something to be eradicated. Therapeutic interventions aimed at autistic people often have the goal of hiding autistic behavior in order to make neurotypical people comfortable – and to keep autistic people safe from non-autistics who might react in suspicious, fearful, and even violent ways to autistic behavior. Often, though, when the central objective is to achieve an adequate performance of neurotypicality, little thought is given to the internal experience of the autist. This is why the first psychiatrist to ever speak to me about autism said there was nothing that could be done to support me even if I was diagnosed because, as he put it, I was already good at holding a 'normal' conversation. He didn't seem to grasp the irony that I was in his office, in tears, because of a lifetime of difficulties brought on, in part, by being an unidentified autistic.

Outside of formal interventions, society at large has its own ways of regulating autistic behavior. As a child, when I was chanting or yelping or yodeling, I can remember hearing taunts calling me ugly names. In this way, many autistic children, even the ones who are undiagnosed or not officially intervened upon, learn to disguise their natural expression, a natural expression that reduces stress, increases concentration, and often provides a feeling of deep contentment in a taxing world.

For me, autistic perception often feels like being unable to filter input. While neurotypical people can usually choose what they focus on – say, a conversation with a friend at a busy cafe –

and let the surrounding din of noise fade into the background, for me this is not always possible. And when it is possible it takes a significant effort and is only possible for a short time. As I focus on what my friend is saying, at the same volume and seeming significance to my perception is the hiss hiss hiss of the milk steamer, the chatter of the other customers, the clank of the waiter stacking dirty plates from the table next to me, the thump of my heartbeat at the base of my neck, the feel of the rough upholstery of the chair I'm sitting on, the click click click of a pen coming from a person writing at a table across the room, the sound of pigeons' rustling wings as they try to build a nest at the top of the window, the thudding drone of traffic, and the tinkle of the bell over the door every time a customer enters.

For me, in these situations, stimming helps my mind sort itself into multiple threads of perception. One thread will be isolated and nimble, able to follow along with the conversation, while others will serve as a throughline to anchor me someplace sensorially more pleasant than the present moment. I will sway back and forth or thrum my fingers rhythmically against my palm, maintaining a connection to a space that can act like a safe container within which I can be held.

For me, stimming can also be an ecstatic practice that opens up new avenues of time, that lets my mind explode into the thousand thousand avenues of perception and language that are native to my way of being, that I yearn to put into a poem, to clap and sniff and blink and think of the meeting of body and not-body as a weird, trembling communion.

41.

I think of six new streets before breakfast. The Earth is a grandee and some of us live here. Be my mind, be still my mind. Catch up with me. Lark for tongues and the taste of bark. A body pressed to wood. I took this from a miser, this coil of an eon. Mind your footfalls when we climb the leaves, this is a way to fall. Dumb heaven has arrived. I snake your chin. I am still thinking of the streets and the shops on the streets and the pour of people from former bodies who are also on the streets. A riptide awakening, that is all. Steal a shovel and dig. Line a casket with patience. The division between wet and dry is new. It alone understands. Water from skin to air and, yes, this is a communion. A damp collar and a tongue for the damp collar. It is every boy ever. The frequency of concentration, the reason for these tremors. I will clap and sniff and blink. You pour laban over ice. We is the way to explain because agreement. The ravish of regret. Steal me. The rhythm is the heartbeat, not the mind. Bigger. Aliens. Steel from stars. A slat for seeing. I peer. Gone. Testament from the before times, before I made a worried thought. She is still wet. She is half-wet and half-dry. It is a comedy for only her. She will do it again. I will do it again. I will clap and sniff and blink. Barks that are not dogs. That is me. I can voice the cats. A string of syllables that spoil the air. The air is getting wet. It is a change for the skin. The skin of my arms is waiting. It is something to anticipate. I have found too many streets and these streets and pouring people. I am already who they were. It is not rhythm, it is a vision. Eyes can pump blood as well as stones. It is in your hand. I am concentrating. It is not ready for explaining. It is the way you sip your drink. My stolen youth had a border around it. Steal another shovel and bury. It is the body of man who was a dog. This week I learned to void. Still I string syllables for the cat. Every boy knows the damp. Awake and wait for aliens. Steel and slats and the wet that dries. Slowly. A shudder beneath clapping. Shake our hands. Lift up the mission. A pool for feet. I will clap and sniff and blink. I voice a tongue that tastes of bark. I voice a body pressed to wood. Dumb heaven for right now. A snake on your chin. In the street I find the rhythm. A pour of caskets. Dead is not dead but only gone.

I peer. A slat for stealing. Explain the argument you made over me. I find no difference in the skin, wet or dry, all is motion. It is the streets and the understand. Barks for testaments and strings. Who they were in a vision for stones. The hand to explain. I do it up again.

42.

Pressure is building within me. Over the past two years of learning about autism this pressure has been growing more insistent, more persistent. I recognize it because it is the same feeling that builds after I've read every book on the library shelf about my latest favorite interest and want – need – to lecture someone about the Inklings or NASA's shuttle era. It feels like lightning has struck the top of my head and is searching searching searching throughout my body for a way out. This is the rhythm of the info-dump, one of the most glorious autistic love languages. What I have learned about autism, about the way it has shaped so much of my life, how it is so much more heterogeneous than the popular clichés would have us believe, is revelatory. I think I am finally ready to share this story with others.

This new story, this story of autism, has shaken the understanding I have held about myself. It came to light because of recurring difficulties throughout my life, difficulties that were revealed to follow a particular pattern, a pattern that meant I could now be described with the word autistic. And, at first, the problems were all that I saw. Problems are what we are given to believe define autism. It is, after all, in medical terminology, a disorder and a disability. And in many ways it can feel disordering because it hinders my ability to follow the patterns set by this world, the patterns that have been neutralized by being defined as normal. But I try to see this, in some ways, as a blessing. There is much about this world

128

that does not make sense to me and I am sometimes glad my efforts to conform myself to it were stymied. And now, through my reading, I have learned that there are an abundance of good things about autism, too, things that make me thrill with recognition, particularly in the way it connects to language.

When I was newly diagnosed it was a story that was too fresh, its roots too fragile to withstand harsh winds, but now it feels more robust. I don't yet know that I understand the story fully, not what autism is, how it factors into my life, or how I feel about it, but I do understand more of it than I did, certainly enough to know that it does merit space within my understanding of myself. And enough to know that I want to finally share this story with others.

Heart in my throat, fingers trembling, I pick up my phone and type out a message to a friend who moved away a couple of years ago and now lives in the foggy green lush of the American Northwest. During the years of our friendship, when we would sip tea while she knitted and her dog snored at our feet, she had spoken to me about having ADHD and the joys and challenges that it brought to her life. I know if anyone would be understanding it would be her.

I hit send and sit back, wondering if what I have done is OK, wondering if by revealing vulnerability a lightning bolt might come out of the sky and smite me.

My friend writes back almost immediately. I see the notification pop up and my heart lurches.

When I tap on the screen, the first thing I see is a 'hug' emoji, a little blip of sweetly smiling yellow. Breath snakes out of me in a long sigh and my shoulders drop from my ears. I read on. Her words are, as I had hoped they would be, full of encouragement and kindness. But her words are also full of something that at first I cannot quite define but later find overwhelmingly touching. Eventually, I realize the quality that suffuses her response is one of equanimity. She understands that being diagnosed shook my life to the core, but in no way has it shaken her perception of me.

To her, I am still the same friend I ever was. She does not treat me any differently, in fact, as the conversation continues across a succession of messages, we are soon off on a tangent, talking about something else entirely.

Buoyed by this positive interaction, a few months later I decide to tell another friend. She lives on a balmy, windswept island in the Atlantic Ocean. In the long, handwritten letters she writes to me it sounds quirky and idyllic, and her perception of the world and of those around her is unfailingly gentle. Though we have not seen one another in person in more than twenty years, such is the strength of her epistolary devotion that I nevertheless feel her presence in my life keenly.

With a twist of nerves in my gut, I send her an email, including, in true autistic fashion, a 1,200 word explanation of what autism can often look like in those who are late-diagnosed and high-masking, as well as some preemptive answers to any question I imagine she might have.

Her response comes the next day. It is joyful, supportive, curious. Understanding this piece of myself, she makes clear, is something wonderful.

In the wake of these conversations with my two friends, I am tender and stunned and grateful. I realize that I have let worry chart my course for too long. Perhaps best of all is the way that my friends continue to treat me just as they always have. I know that isn't a given, that there will be people who will react negatively, but to start in this manner makes the ground beneath my feet feel solid. There are things about every one of us that don't quite add up to what we are told is 'normal', ways in which we all feel, at times, like we just don't fit. Having a story to make sense of this for myself has made me, finally, able to forgive myself for floundering when I thought I had no right to flounder. In telling my friends this new story of self, it is beginning to feel more settled, less outsized, more like something than can be approached from a myriad of directions. It is becoming a landscape that feels familiar.

43. Saar, Bahrain, 2016

Summer solstice and the path of the sun and the pits where the Dilmuns made their beer. Dust. Dust in the sky and in my eyes and in my nose. Dust cloaking the broken mounds of the archeological site. In every inhalation, the smell of atomized earth. The smell of forgotten places and forgotten people and the dirty job of remembering.

The archeologist who invited us here is standing down in one of the pits, explaining the beer-making process, which involved wheat and water and feet. I am already scanning the sky, worrying that we will miss what we have come here for.

The archeologist's theory about the summer solstice – that it marked the beginning of the Dilmun year – is not fact but conjecture. All of us gathered here today have come on the basis of his supposition. His theory could be true, and it could not be true, and in an hour or so the sun will follow its curious solstice path into an ancient temple and we will all reach our own conclusions.

Right now the sun is a mealy yolk hanging over a batch of spiky buildings in the distance. The sky itself has faded to its traditional summer pallor. Next to the spiky high-rises next to the archeological site there is a bulky mega-mart and next to that is a multiscreen cinema and next to that is a village of low, pale houses and listless palm trees. On the wind is the scent of burning rubbish and distant salt shores baked hard in the sun.

It is Ramadan and none of the Muslims in the group have had food or water since sun-up. It is not acceptable for anyone, including non-Muslims, to eat or drink in public during daylight hours. The high today was nearly fifty degrees centigrade, and the humidity so stifling that my jeans are stuck to my legs like soggy towels. Among the crowd, I notice more than a few sidelong glances toward the boxes of water stacked along one ancient wall, waiting to be broken into as soon as sunset prayer rings out from the mosques surrounding us in all directions.

A Filipino couple holds their toddler between them, each clutching one of her chubby fists. Two young people wearing T-shirts from a Scottish university are following the archeologist's every word, asking questions by raising their hands, like we are all in class together. A Japanese student is tapping into his phone. A Bahraini man stifles a yawn.

Movement.

In the distance, something shifts between earth and sky.

A tiny point twists in on itself.

A clot – a welt – an abrasion.

A broken place amid the symmetry.

I squint, but the sun is too bright. Whatever it is, it is moving toward us quickly even though the earth is littered with thorny bushes and broken car fenders and tangles of barbed wire.

The movement finally breaks free from its shroud of sunlight and becomes visible. It is a human figure. It is a woman dressed in white. I see white hair and I know it is an old woman. Closer she comes and I can see sloping shoulders, clenched hands, and the pale, fish-belly skin of her throat.

She circles the crowd, then comes closer and stops. No one else seems to have noticed her. I turn to the woman in white and smile.

'You are walking on the dead.' She says it flatly, so that I think I've misheard. Then she repeats herself. 'You are walking on the dead.'

Her voice is strange, with an accent I can't place.

'Actually,' I say, 'the archeologist explained that the graveyard is some distance away. This is where people lived. That was a pit where they made beer.'

The woman in white continues, 'Dilmun was the Land of the Living. The dead were once alive.'

The archeologist gestures to the crowd and heads down the path. The crowd follows. I follow, thinking that the dead *were* once alive. The dead were once alive and the dead were once alive *here*.

There are no plaques or guidebooks or displays, nothing but an excavated site of dirt lanes, unearthed buildings, and low, broken walls. Without the archeologist to lead the way, I would be unable to recognize anything. He moves quickly, excited, leading us to a stone building with two rooms that are not much larger than closets.

'4,000 years ago this was someone's home,' he says, as we all step over the ankle-high walls into the space. 'The cooking was done here, and here is where we think they slept. Probably the parents in this corner and any children they had in the other.'

People are taking photos, whispering to one another, nodding.

The woman in white stands some distance away, across the dirt lane from the house, gazing up the hill. Despite the dust, her white clothes – blouse, slacks, loafers – are pristine, like she hasn't been walking through the same desert as the rest of us. Following her eyes, I realize she is looking in the direction of the temple, where this solstice tour will end.

The archeologist leads us from place to place. With his explanation, nondescript piles of rubble become homes and storage rooms and kitchens and wells. We learn about Dilmun farming practices and their distinctive pottery. We learn about their family life and diet and construction methods. My mind drifts. I think of the preparations taking place now in all the houses in the neighborhoods that surround this site. I think of the kitchens full of vine leaves, fragrant rice, roasting lamb, raisins, saffron, cumin, and syrupy kunafa. I think of grandmothers stuffing pinches of onions and beef into hollowed-out zucchini, children sneaking into the kitchen to marvel, uncles and cousins on plastic-covered couches rubbing their hands and eyeing the clock. Everyone hungry, everyone waiting.

Coming up next to me, the woman in white whispers, 'Do you know about the water chambers? The God of the Abyss?'

I look around. The archeologist is talking about an oven and bread and the fecundity of Bahraini soil. Everyone is listening to him so no one else seems to hear the darting whispers of this woman.

Before I reply, she goes on, 'The Dilmun god Enki was lord of the freshwater sea – and of wisdom and creation and magic. Enki's domain was in the watery abyss beneath the world and the Dilmuns built shrines so they could speak to him.'

'The Barbar Temple?' I ask.

'There are secret things in the earth,' she says, 'in the land, that want to be told. They rise up *through* us. In these ancient stories, long ago Bahrain did not have the freshwater springs it has now. It was barren and dry until Enki ordered the land to have fresh water and it did.'

She continues, painting a scene so vivid with damp stone and hushed underground echoes that I almost feel I can step into her words and vanish from the heat of the surrounding day. She tells me how these dark chambers were a sacred threshold between the subterranean world of the gods and the terrestrial world of humans. In this in-between space, the Dilmuns believed they could work the most powerful magics. She describes supplicants making their way to the temple, carrying offerings of copper and dates, warm wine and goats' cheese. They spoke to their gods, they beseeched them, they prayed for abundant crops and good health. They left behind the world of the living, of mundane sunlight and blue skies, walking out of the brightness and into the dark, venturing into a liminal space where man could speak and gods would listen.

The woman in white goes quiet and before I can decide what to say to her she is walking away from me. I watch her spare white figure move down the path, so focused on the precise movement of her small feet against the dry earth that it takes me a moment to realize the whole group is walking, too. The archeologist is bounding ahead of us, pointing at the setting sun. The time has come to visit the temple.

The temple sits at the top of a low rise. It is small and deeply sunken into the earth. At the urging of the archeologist, we all sit down onto the hard, rocky ground and dangle our legs into the space – and then we jump.

I land hard and steady myself against a rough, crumbling wall – a wall that is 4,000 years old and that I probably shouldn't be touching. But then I look around and realize everyone has their hands outstretched, fingertips tracing the rough pale stone. Down here, within this basin of earth, sound is muffled. There is a line of massive stone columns running through the center of the space and along one pale wall there is a jutting altar of stone topped by a crescent moon carved out of rock.

The archeologist turns to the group and begins to speak. Twenty years ago, he tells us, he was working on the site as it was still being excavated. After a long day, he collected his tools, stretched his back, and, out of the corner of his eye, noticed something. The steady glare of the setting sun was wobbling. As he recounts this story, he animates this wobbling of the sun by lifting his hand to his face and waving his fingers in a waterfall motion. He says he realized the sun's light was being caught precisely in the corner of the temple.

He leads us now to a doorway. Through the doorway is a small, triangular-shaped room, only large enough to hold a few people. Shoulders jostle against shoulders, bodies bump bodies, as everyone pushes for a glimpse.

Peeking inside, I see it – the sun, almost set, is hovering over the corner of the room. It is slightly off-kilter now, so many thousands of years after the temple was built on shifting sand, but the alignment is uncanny.

Murmuring from the crowd. People grab for their phones to take pictures. The sun, which moves so slowly when perched high in the sky, is now rubbing against the horizon and descending swiftly. In silence, we watch it fall.

We are standing in a space where, perhaps, thousands of years ago temple priests stood to mark time. It was a way for them to understand the processes of the natural world. A conversation, if you will, held at the end of one Dilmun year and the beginning of the next. Thousands of years have passed and the sun is still moving through this narrow alcove. Thousands of years have passed and we are still gathering here to watch. We are speaking now to the world as the once-alive Dilmuns spoke to the world. We have done our part by coming here, by standing in the desert in the heat and the dust, and the sun is doing its part by falling toward the Earth.

But, this isn't entirely true. In truth, we are witnessing the movement of the Earth in relation to the sun. It is those of us gathered here today who are moving. Spinning through space on the arc of the Earth's orbital path, today reaching our closest point to the sun before, tomorrow, hurtling away once again. We have not only come here to witness the sun, we have come here to witness ourselves.

It is over quickly. We stare at the bleeding red edge that is left behind on the horizon for a long time, no one wanting to break the spell. I am suddenly keenly aware of how close I am standing to the strangers around me. I can feel every movement of them – the bend of an elbow, the sway of a knee.

And then, from across the island, comes a wave of noise. It lifts up from every direction, as hundreds of muezzins in hundreds of mosques begin the call to prayer. The sun has set, the day is over, fasting is done.

We clamber out of the temple. My body feels watery, unwieldy, and it takes me several tries to heave myself up and out over the scrim of earth. There is the sound of cardboard boxes being torn open and a warm bottle of water is pressed into my hand. Two fasting men open tins of dates and offer them to everyone before taking any for themselves. When I put the date between my teeth I find it sticky and sweet as molasses. Then comes the smell of dark coffee and green cardamom. Two men roll out rugs directly onto the ground and many gather to pray. Everywhere is laughter. We offer one another toasts and well wishes – happy new year is cheered.

I look around for the woman in white but cannot see her anywhere. But then – a curl of movement. Melting across the desert, a column of white. She hasn't disappeared, she has just left. I watch her walking across the desert as the fierce daylight fades from the sky and colors – plum and scarlet and blue – return to the world. I watch her as a spinning cloud of gulls wheels overhead. I watch her until the clot, the moving abrasion of her, rejoins the fine line of the horizon and is gone.

44.

These are the words I keep coming back to as I walk through cities and souqs and shopping malls and nascent industrial sites and shabby seaside shisha cafes and heritage villages and vegetable markets and sheep markets and luxury car dealers and high-end compounds and museums and galleries and cold stores: divergent, weird, warped, crooked.

As I walk I am a roving point in space that is dependent on the street, informed by the street, mediated by the street. This I have long known. But I am starting to understand that I am just as porous as everything else, which means, as I walk and drift and rove through the streets, the streets around me are dependent on me, informed by me, mediated by me.

The streets, I am beginning to recognize, have their own secret something.

45.

We were born here so we know how to do. This is the way you walk when you walk. An engine of engines. A glitter of glitter.

At the corniche we gather, men to one side, women to the other, children drifting between, to watch the constellation of Earth. Force and proclivity, tingle and strip, all the whole day is before me. Also, it is not yours.

The departure of myth is something we count – a tickbox for each missing hour. Any memory not capitulated is likely to re-form. It is forsaken, this tally. The formation of expatriates requires a mobile constitution, a tendency to ruminate, and general indemnity from causes. A coalition of glass bottles rolling up a hill.

Every sentence means more than the last. The last flight before the war, the first flight after. Gas masks and lunchboxes and toys from West Berlin. Stamps on every page are a pale substitute for personality. At the juncture a patient mausoleum, not in fact, but in kind. A barbershop television holds an ardah troupe, a swing of blinding men. Hands are pressed to hearts. A hundred slanting houses and the people that fill them.

Windows are watching the way that we pass, windows that were originally a kind of freedom. In a building of basements we wait for captive fish. There is salt, much of it, in the air we breathe. A lace of weather collects the skull.

When women were able to drive, we drove. When women were able to sit, we sat. There are no windows in the room where I am allowed, in the room where I order herbs and labneh. All is yellow. All is a pension for tomorrow. There is a bridge to cross that requires courage. In any direction, traffic. A wild dog with terrible teats, murals of cats and fish and authentic girls of the shrouded kind.

If a study is made of forgiveness, a want of thrift will be found. Gifts of old chocolate for those not with child, fat ribbons of serge. A majlis for old men, electricity provided, and a shy boy to bring tea. Posters from Eid, and the Eid before.

At night, we gather on plastic for chicken and rice. Behind the mosque, the cigarette store. Behind the mosque, a park for dolphins. Women and nannies and children and fog. At the bright shop we huddle for juice, we spin the fat meat and watch the drip. A lengthy discussion about our gift for departure.

Again, a reality. It is a city of choices. Of noise. It is a certainty of imported glitter. A squat hotel named for my kin. A tower named for my sign. The darkened heft of a feasible edge. The windows, same as before, bear witness: cover your roots before leaving.

46.

I walk and I think of how often I have heard, over the years, that my writing is strange, crooked, unexpected, divergent, how it carves weird paths and veers in odd directions. Walking through the city, thinking these thoughts, I imagine the traces I have left along the streets, the rogue trajectories of my path, the shimmering memories that linger, and I imagine the rambling web I have made.

I am realizing that all of this time my psychogeography has been autistic. It has been an autistic reckoning of space and place, an autistic sense of the street beyond the street. Walking, I think of my crooked thoughts and my wayward trails and I think of the prefix skolio – from a Greek word that means crooked or diverging – and I join it to the word geography – also from Greek, meaning earth writing. I walk and I think of skoliogeography, an autistic psychogeography; a psychogeography that gives preeminence to autistic ways of being and doing and seeing and writing. A psychogeography that resists ossified methodology – no confluence, no skoliogeography. Better to say skoliogeographies, perhaps, because there is not one, but many.

47.

Skoliogeography is faithfully open, permeable, endlessly adaptable. Skoliogeography also knows the value of roots. It is untranslated autistic experience, it lives in the crackling electricity of the skin, where it can exist shorn of motive or framework. Skoliogeography is autistic consciousness on the page, but it is a consciousness that is, at all times, emerging. Skoliogeography is solipsistic precisely because I am not entirely a separate being; I am a filament of creation. I am, in fact, a point of departure.

48.

Skoliogeography is understanding that for autistics walking and wandering are often viewed as pathological, yet another indicator of abnormality. Skoliogeography, then, is a subversion of non-autistic understandings of what it means to move through space. In this, skoliogeography takes the understanding of the barzakh, as a place where things are brought together yet are simultaneously held apart, and applies this to motion – of bodies and of thought and of the self – in relation to place. In the liquidity of interrelation, skoliogeography seeks the fundamental rhythm.

49.

Skoliogeography is knowing the mythic value of repetition – that if you look again and again you will find the broken piece of glory. Once is rarely ever enough and multiple approaches reveal new vistas and fresh stories. Skoliogeography is knowing, too, the value of echolalia, which is the thingness of language, which is the recognition that sometimes the newest thing that can be said is the oldest, and in this way hordes of meaning can be made.

50.

Skoliogeography is an orthogonal approach to place. As an implementation of the autistic gaze, skoliogeography is something that can be found within a street, within the walker on the street, and within the text produced by the walker on the street. As an aesthetic it is bound by liquid borders and open to all.

Skoliogeography is not just seeking the marvelous in the mundane, but expecting it.

51.

I am going to the cornice because I am always going to the cornice. But, then, diversion: in the butcher's window, the gloss of a goat's gelatinous eye and the reflection of electricity fizzing from streetlights that should have gone dead at dawn. In the shop next door, mannequins jamble the doorway, their faces carved away to stained Styrofoam nothings. And, up above, the punch-drunk blue of the noonday sky.

Into a courtyard teeming with pigeons, into a courtyard hazy with bukhoor, into a courtyard thick with a watery sort of sunlight. My mind, already following a thousand thousand trails of sensory input, fragments: the sunlight is the sunlight before a rain shower/the bukhoor is cheap and too sweet along the edges/the pigeons coo and their coos form a cottony softness that hovers like fog.

I don't think these thoughts in quick succession; I think these thoughts simultaneously. The world around me feels as if it is thickening, meaning gathers and coheres so that everything I see distracts me with its significance.

Ragged clouds are now making their way in from off-shore and the face of the city goes mottled in the sudden shadow. I smell rain and I smell the shadow itself, the heavy, limpid weight of it. There is expectation in the air; the crowd is on the brink of giddiness; if I could find the right word I think I could set this whole street off.

I count eleven cracks in the ruptured pavement, each one spiraling its own course toward the sea. The cornice, I am still heading to the cornice, but I seem to have lost my way. The street has changed: it was the gloss in the goat's eye, the loud blue of the sky, that did it. I can still hear the blue ringing in my ears. I stumble and I veer. Today the city is conspiring, beguiling, banging drums of myth and memory. I count again the eleven cracks and, unsteadily numbered, move on.

52. Dammam, Saudi Arabia, 2022

The silence of the jebels is a Friday occasion. Before Jummah, before the jets begin, before the panting of wayward dogs and the puffing of their red-faced owners, the early Friday silence of the jebels is a magisterial event, a rousing elemental thunder behind the lids. When I open my eyes, the world is still there, startling and wide and waiting.

The silence of the jebels on a Friday morning isn't silent, though. There are constant eruptions of small birds from windblown bushes – the sleek brown darting of desert finches, the gaiety of bulbuls, and the ghostly whistle of the hoopoe. There is also the wind, the scuttle of rocks underfoot, and the laconic see-saw buzz of some kind of insect I can always hear but never quite see. The silence, then, is only of the human variety, a specific texture of stillness that feels like it adds space and depth to the immensity of landscape.

There is a rough track that runs away from the road and the parking lot to scoop around the smaller jebels and ravel up the biggest – a narrow path defined by it having slightly fewer rocks than the surrounding land. Along each side are thorn bushes, acacia trees, and gatherings of spiky desert hyacinth. I make my way along this track until I reach the jebel I have told myself I will climb.

I am halfway up, my fingers dusted by the sharp rocks I grab to hold myself steady, before I realize it is too hot to be out here today. Already my heart is pounding and my skin feels tight as a drum; if I am not careful I know I will have a headache later.

Quick then, I'll be quick. I move faster, pushing off of rocks that aren't entirely steady, scrabbling up the jebel's patient face. All I want, all I need, is a few minutes at the top, a few minutes to sit and see the world spread out beneath me, because this is a day of spinning words and sunbeams like scalpels, a day for making sense of journeys.

When I do reach the top, a flat expanse of wind-bedraggled bushes and canting, crumbling boulders, I walk the circumference of the jebel's edge, catching my breath. From a sky drained of color by the fierce heat the sun beats down on me and beads of sweat roll down my forehead and into my eyes. Out of the corner of my vision, I catch sight of the frantic scramble of a lizard darting for cover beneath rocks, his pale, translucent body vanishing the moment I turn to follow his path. There are, in the jebels, countless places for soft bodies to hide. Sometimes, when I'm out here walking, I find the skeletal remains of cats and tiny desert mice, their bones sharply white in the desert haze.

I am nowhere near the true wild – from the top of this jebel in one direction I can see the square green stamp of a soccer field, where occasionally the local Girl Scout and Boy Scout troops set up Bedouin tents and camp for the weekend. Beyond the soccer field are miles of red-roofed neighborhoods with their frangipani-lined streets. In the other direction, there are office buildings and industrial lots where cranes and bulldozers are stabled. If I squint, on a clear day, I can see in the far distance the tricky mirror-like sheen of the sea.

Immediately to my right is a sprawling jebel where a keen-eyed, golden-faced trickster lives. This fox often watches me walk past from his high perch, trotting around the jebel after me with his plume of a tail trailing him like a shadow, keeping abreast of my comings and goings. He has stories to tell, and I believe the jebels listen. The stray dogs that sometimes make their way through here, scared and hungry, have their stories to tell, too. The honey buzzards that circle up against the face of the sky, dipping their golden wings left and right to soar or sink, I know they, too, have their stories. The nimble hedgehogs, the bright sweet acacia, the scudding dragonflies, the wadi waiting half a year for rain – stories, all of them. As mythologist Martin Shaw suggests, the stories we humans tell are not just for human ears; indeed, many of them did not even arise just from human minds. Some stories, Shaw contends, are not told by humans but *through* humans.[62] Walking in the desert I cannot help but wonder what stories have been told through me.

Amid the towering grandeur of the jebels I feel inconsequentially small, a fleeting animal presence in the shadow of their eon-spanning gaze. This awareness brings with it a wild wonder so potent that it fills my body like the frothing edge of a curling wave. I am not as singular or unique as I sometimes think I am – and how wonderful it is to know that. The stories I want to tell are informed by this awareness, by this need to outline the mercurial and the transient so that I can more clearly see the eternal. There have been an immeasurable number of stories before mine and there will surely be an immeasurable number of stories after. Feeling like a curling wave here, like one aspect of an unthinkable multitude, feels apt. In the desert, I am always confronted with the truth that there is no certain way for the finite to express the infinite; there is only sitting down at the edge of a jebel to rest in this particular moment and feel its reverberations.

When I listen closely here, among the jebels, I often think I can hear whispers of other ways of knowing. I like to think that stories are rooted in place, in the way that dandelions are rooted: they grow up from the soil, saturated with the essence of their native land, but once they have fully bloomed, their seeds scatter and travel for miles on the wind. In this view, stories have a way of defying borders that feels verdant with possibility. Of course, I like this notion because it makes space for someone like me to feel a kinship to the place I call home, a kinship that goes deeper than nationality, language, or human-made culture.

I often wonder what it means that I belong to places I can never fully claim. Even after all this time I'm not sure I know with any certainty. It has been fifteen years since I last visited the United States – my passport country – and when I was there it never did manage to feel like home. Yet here in the Gulf, where I do feel a sense of belonging, I have no centuries of ancestors to call upon who knew this land, and therefore I know there are those who would say I have no right to call it home. But I do sometimes get a sense of being recognized here in the jebels, as if the jebels themselves know that I have been seeking refuge in their shadows for the last forty years. As if maybe they somehow understand what it is they mean to me. In the scope of their existence, sixty-three million years and counting, forty years isn't much, just the merest blink of time, but I know how meaningful blinks can be and I hope that just as the jebels mean so much to me, that, in turn, it might be possible that I mean something to them.

In recent years, I have spent more time than ever here in the desert, scrambling up and down the dusty tracks of these jebels, often alone but never lonely. The stories still told about autism say that it causes profound isolation, which, considering the many ways in which society is still unwelcoming to those who are autistic, is true for many. But, for some, autism can, at the very same time, also feel like a vast, turbulent awareness of the self's essential connection to everyone and everything – a sense of connection that can fly in the face of what we are told is proper. Too often we are encouraged to wallow in the kind of solipsism that I would argue is the opposite of autistic consciousness, the kind that does not see the self as a doorway to the all, but the kind that sees the self *as* the all.

We modern humans long ago stamped out the crackling, luminous campfires of myth, telling ourselves that without these 'superstitions' we would finally know the clean peace of rational thought. Instead, with nothing to light the way for our deeper selves, we now fumble through self-inflicted darkness. In the resulting sterile isolation we are unable to imagine other minds, other ways of being in this world, and we make up smaller stories, meager tales that cannot bear the weight we need them to bear, that in their very telling dismiss our aching need for meaning. Eventually, with nothing left to believe in, we are left with only the self, and so we make an eternal project of parsing our differences and determining our supposed separation from others. But, the further I have gone toward trying to understand the new story of autism and the way it makes sense of my life, the more the self seems a nebulous thing, something to pass beyond rather than linger permanently within. Maybe we are meant to learn the ways that we are different so that we may ultimately better learn the ways in which we can come together.

Learning that I am autistic, which is perhaps one of the stories that can today be said to describe me, has helped me to understand some of the more difficult aspects of my life, but I am aware of the sticky allure of hardship. I want to retain my awareness that there are any number of paths to take, horizons to seek, stories to tell. I used to think skoliogeography could help me to write these new stories that could make sense of these thoughts, but, increasingly, skoliogeography guides me back to some of the oldest stories of all, revealing that whatever supposedly new thing I wanted to say has been said before, again and again, in a myriad of ways. Shaw writes that the stories that we need arrived thousands of years ago, and I find myself heart-pulled by the truth of that notion.[63] It is certainly the old stories that I need, stories already richly veined with the knowledge of how to slip skins and become the jebel fox, the soaring honey buzzard, the thirsting wadi waiting for rain. These are stories that already know the self as a portal, both fearfully and wonderfully made, embedded in a cosmos resplendent with meaning. There is beauty, these stories teach, wild beauty, in the world as it is right now all around us. The miraculous alongside the mundane, meaning in every motion.

There are some stories that, once you hear them, change the way you see the world, like a smear of enchanted earth thumbed across your eye by one of the fair folk. These stories are often about slipping beyond the bounds of what we thought we knew, venturing into the perilous realm, and returning, mussed and scarred, clutching tightly to our hard-won boon. Once you have experienced the world from a storied perspective, it is impossible to forget. You can never again see a street as only a street; it will forever be a site suffused with the most marvelous apprehension of meaning. Because, for all my veering, I do believe there is a truth and that perhaps it can best be found in the weird dreams of a more real world and the knowledge that the closer we are to paradox, the closer we may be to revelation. There is a street beyond the street and on it we may drift toward the sublime.

Let us see where it might lead.

53. Dhahran, Saudi Arabia, 2018

In a long arc-shaped room in the basement of the museum, there is a towering globe. With the smooth slide of a lever, the globe will spin and flash, depicting the geological processes that formed the Arabian landmass over the past 500 million years. I push the lever and landmasses dance and melt before me, shifting with the permutations of volcanoes, tectonic plates, and the slip of ancient oceans.

I spend hours in this room. I walk circuits. I watch families come and go, I nod at the shy guard, I do not want to leave. Always I return to the globe where landmasses disassemble, re-forming to take the places they occupied 443 million years ago, when the Arabian Peninsula was near the bottom of the planet, part of a continent known as Gondwana. Eventually, Gondwana and neighboring continent Euramerica collide, creating the single world continent, Pangea. I watch as 200 million years pass, and the landmass that will become the Arabian Peninsula undulates across the globe to settle, partly underwater, near the equator.

Then, twenty-three million years ago, as the Red Sea Rift drives apart the African Plate and the Arabian Plate, I watch the creation of the Red Sea, with a sudden, sloshing influx of water. And then it is two and a half million years ago and, on the other side of the Peninsula, there is an emergence. From the depths of the ocean, the eastern perimeter of Saudi Arabia begins to appear, revealing the outline of the landmass I know so well. I wait for the swell of coastline where I am, and it is one of the last features to emerge.

Next to the globe is a two-dimensional map laid out on a circular stand. Here, you can watch the interplay of Saudi Arabia's deserts: An Nafud Al Kabir in the north, birthplace of massive sandstorms; the slender corridor of Ad Dahna in the center of the country, linking the three; and in the south, the great Ar Rub' Al Khali, the largest continuous sand desert in the world, with dunes as big as mountains.

Given strong enough winds to drive sand particles, dunes can migrate. They become so steep that they collapse under their own weight, sending cascades of falling sand from the top to the bottom where they slowly pile up. A sand dune can travel like this, collapsing and re-forming, collapsing and re-forming, for miles. And, if a migrating dune crosses paths with another sand dune, they can even reproduce, breaking apart to multiply and re-form anew.

The same land, but never the same. The only constant, change.

Endnotes

5.

1 Yergeau, M Remi, *Authoring Autism: On Rhetoric and Neurological Queerness*, Duke University Press: Durham and London, 2018, pp.7–12

2 Ibid.

6.

3 Nadesan, Majia Holmer, *Constructing Autism: Unraveling the 'truth' and understanding the social*, Routledge: New York and London, 2005, p.9

4 Yergeau, M Remi, *Authoring Autism: On Rhetoric and Neurological Queerness*, Duke University Press: Durham and London, 2018, p.43

7. Manama, Bahrain, 2017

5 Dagnino, Arianna, *Transcultural Writers and Novels in the Age of Global Mobility*, Purdue University Press: West Lafayette, 2015, p.70

6 Trojanow, Ilija, and Hoskote, Ranjit, *Kampfabsage*, Karl Blessing Verlag GmbH: Munich, 2007, pp.4–5

7 Ibid., p.7

11. Thuqbah, Saudi Arabia, 2018

8 Aragon, Louis, *Paris Peasant*, trans. Simon Watson Taylor, Exact Change: Cambridge, 1994, p.11

9 Khatib, Abdelhafid (1958). 'Attempt at a Psychogeographical Description of Les Halles.' *Internationale Situationniste #2* December, trans. Paul Hammond, *Situationist International Online* https://isinenglish.com/is-2

10 Smith, Phil, *Mythogeography: A Guide to Walking Sideways*, Triarchy Press: Charmouth, 2010, p.113

11 Richardson, Tina, 'Developing Schizocartography: Formulating a Theoretical Methodology for a Walking Practice' in *Walking Inside Out: Contemporary British Psychogeography* ed. Tina Richardson, Rowman & Littlefield: London, 2015, p.182

12 Wark, McKenzie, *The Beach Beneath the Street: The Everyday Life and Glorious Times of the Situationist International*, Verso: London, 2015, p.22

12.

13 Hendrickx, Sarah, *Women and Girls with Autism Spectrum Disorder: Understanding Life Experiences from Early Childhood to Old Age*, Jessica Kingsley Publishers: London, 2015, p.22

14 Ibid., p.25

15 McCrossin, Robert (2022). 'Finding the True Number of Females with Autistic Spectrum Disorder by Estimating the Biases in Initial Recognition and Clinical Diagnosis.' *Children* 9, 272. https://www.mdpi.com/2227-9067/9/2/272

16 Yergeau, M Remi, *Authoring Autism: On Rhetoric and Neurological Queerness*, Duke University Press: Durham and London, 2018, p.47

13.

17 www.planetneurodivergent.com/the-diagnosis-trap-jim-hoerricks-phd

16. Riyadh, Saudi Arabia, 1994

18 Al-Naim, Mashary A, 'Riyadh: A City of "Institutional" Architecture' in *The Evolving Arab City: Tradition, Modernity and Urban Development* ed. Yasser Elsheshtawy, Routledge: Oxford and New York, 2011, p.124

19 Meier, Sandra M, et al. (2015). 'Obsessive-Compulsive Disorder and Autism Spectrum Disorders: Longitudinal and Offspring

Risk.' *PloS one* vol. 10,11 e0141703. https://doi.org/10.1371/journal.pone.0141703

20 Wikramanayake, Waduge Nishani Maheshi, Mandy, William, Shahper, Sonia, Kaur, Sukhwinder, Kolli, Sangeetha, Osman, Selma, Reid, Jemma, Jefferies-Sewell, Kiri, Fineberg, Naomi Anne (2018). 'Autism spectrum disorders in adult outpatients with obsessive compulsive disorder in the UK.' *International Journal of Psychiatry in Clinical Practice*, 22(1):54 – 62. https://pubmed.ncbi.nlm.nih.gov/28705096

17. Dhahran, Saudi Arabia, 2000

21 www.chadd.org/about-adhd/adhd-and-autism-spectrum-disorder

22 van der Meer, Jolanda M J, Oerlemans, Anoek M, van Steijn, Daphne J, Lappenschaar, Martijn G A, de Sonneville, Leo M J, Buitelaar, Jan K, Rommelse, Nanda N J (2012). 'Are autism spectrum disorder and attention-deficit/hyperactivity disorder different manifestations of one overarching disorder? Cognitive and symptom evidence from a clinical and population-based sample.' *Journal of the American Academy of Child and Adolescent Psychiatry*, 51(11):1160-1172 https://pubmed.ncbi.nlm.nih.gov/23101742

18. London, England, 2001

23 Machen, Arthur, *N*, Snuggly Books, 2018

24 www.autism.org.uk/advice-and-guidance/topics/mental-health/anxiety

25 www.planetneurodivergent.com/creativity-functioning-skills-rethinking-executive-dysfunction

19. Oakville, Texas, USA, 2003

26 Van Reken, Ruth E, 'Cross-Cultural Kids: The New Prototype' in *Writing out of Limbo: International Childhoods, Global Nomads and Third Culture Kids*, ed. Gene H. Bell-Villada, Nina Sichel, Faith Eidse, and Elaine Neil Orr, Cambridge Scholars: Newcastle upon Tyne, 2013, p.38

20. Abu Saiba, Bahrain, 2007

27 www.healthline.com/health/autism/autism-masking#autism

28 www.sprc.org/news/suicide-risk-among-people-autism-spectrum-disorder

25.

29 Dagnino, Arianna, *Transcultural Writers and Novels in the Age of Global Mobility*, Purdue University Press: West Lafayette, 2015, p.162

26. Seef, Bahrain, 2019

30 Vora, Neha, *Impossible Citizens: Dubai's Indian Diaspora*, Duke University Press: Durham and London, 2013, p.53

31 Abdulkarim, Khaled A (2017). 'Crystallizing a Discourse of "Khalijiness": Exclusion and Citizenship in the Arab Gulf States.' *CUREJ: College Undergraduate Research Electronic Journal*, University of Pennsylvania, May 15, p.50 https://repository.upenn.edu/curej/211

32 www.thecommononline.org/introduction-portfolio-of-writing-from-the-arabian-gulf

33 Vora, Neha, *Impossible Citizens: Dubai's Indian Diaspora*, Duke University Press: Durham and London, 2013, p.115

28. Manama, Bahrain, 2018

34 Fuccaro, Nelida, *Histories of City and State in the Persian Gulf: Manama since 1800*, Cambridge University Press: Cambridge, 209, pp.62–67

35 Rodenbeck, Max (2008). 'The Early Days' in *The New York Times*, January 6

36 Berry, Ellen E, and Epstein, Mikhail N, *Transcultural Experiments: Russian and American Models of Creative Communication*, St. Martin's Press: New York, 1999, pp.3, 9, 25

37 Ibid., p.94

38 Welsch, Wolfgang (2001). 'Transculturality: The Changing Form of Cultures Today.' *Filozofski vestnik*, letnik vol. XXII, No. 2, pp.59–86

39 Dagnino, Arianna, *Transcultural Writers and Novels in the Age of Global Mobility*, Purdue University Press: West Lafayette, 2015, p.190

31. Khobar, Saudi Arabia, 2021

40 Al-Ghadeer, Moneera, *Desert Voices*, Tauris Academic Studies: New York, 2009

41 Cole, Donald P (2003). 'Where Have the Bedouin Gone?' *Anthropological Quarterly*, vol. 76, no. 2, Spring, p.248

42 Ibid., pp.237–243

43 Al-Ghadeer, Moneera, *Desert Voices*, Tauris Academic Studies: New York, 2009, pp.150–152

44 Ibid.

45 Ibid., p.96

32.

46 Brinkmann, Svend (2017). 'Perspectives on diagnosed suffering.' *Nordic Psychology*, 69:1, 1-4. https://doi.org/10.1080/19012276.2016.1270404

47 Nadesan, Majia Holmer, *Constructing Autism: Unraveling the 'truth' and understanding the social*, Routledge: New York and London, 2005, pp.5–9

48 Walker, Nick, *Neuroqueer Heresies*, Autonomous Press: Fort Worth, 2021, pp.34–39, 58–59

49 Ibid., p.74

50 Shaw, Martin, *Scatterlings: Getting Claimed in the Age of Amnesia*, White Cloud Press: Ashland, 2016, p.9

33. Muharraq, Bahrain, 2022

51 May, Katherine, *The Electricity of Every Living Thing: A Woman's Walk in the Wild to Find Her Way Home*, Orion: London, 2018, p.81

52 Savarese, Ralph James (2012). 'River of Words, Raft of Our Conjoined Neurologies.' *Fourth Genre*, vol. 14, no. 1, Spring, pp.43–52

34. Karanah, Bahrain, 2018

53 Dagnino, Arianna, *Transcultural Writers and Novels in the Age of Global Mobility*, Purdue University Press: West Lafayette, 2015, p.94

38.

54 Savarese, Ralph James (2010). 'Toward a Postcolonial Neurology: Autism, Tito Mukhopadhyay, and a New Geo-poetics of the Body.' *Journal of Literary and Cultural Disability Studies* 4(3) 273-290 https://doi.org/10.1057/9781137363787_7

55 Yergeau, M Remi, *Authoring Autism: On Rhetoric and Neurological Queerness*, Duke University Press: Durham and London, 2018, p.16

56 www.lithub.com/the-listening-world-neurodivergent-voices-for-a-more-than-human-world

57 Rodas, Julia Miele, *Autistic Disturbances: Theorizing Autism Poetics from the DSM to Robinson Crusoe*, University of Michigan Press: Ann Arbor, 2018, p.34

58 Brown, Julie, *Writers on the Spectrum: How Autism and Asperger Syndrome Have Influenced Literary Writing*, Jessica Kingsley Publishers: London, 2010, pp.15–16, 20–22, 27, 32, 38, 208

59 Rodas, Julia Miele, *Autistic Disturbances: Theorizing Autism Poetics from the DSM to Robinson Crusoe*, University of Michigan Press: Ann Arbor, 2018, pp.2–3

60 Yergeau, M Remi (2018). 'Foreword' in *Autistic Disturbances: Theorizing Autism Poetics from the DSM to Robinson Crusoe*, Rodas, Julia Miele, University of Michigan Press: Ann Arbor, 2018, p.x

39.

61 Yergeau, M Remi, *Authoring Autism: On Rhetoric and Neurological Queerness*, Duke University Press: Durham and London, 2018, p.38

52. Dammam, Saudi Arabia, 2022

62 Shaw, Martin, *A Branch from the Lightning Tree: Ecstatic Myth and the Grace in Wildness*, White Cloud Press: Ashland, 2011), p.xx

63 www.drmartinshaw.com/essays

Original sources and permissions

Grateful thanks to Deepak Unnikrishnan for permission to quote from 'Introduction: Portfolio of Writing from the Arabian Gulf' which appeared in *The Common*, online, 2021.

Thank you to Bloomsbury for permission to quote from *Desert Voices*, © Moneera Al-Ghadeer, Tauris Academic Studies, New York, 2009.

Permission has been granted to use the quotes from *Autistic Disturbances* © Julia Miele Rodas, University of Michigan Press, Ann Arbor, 2018.

Acknowledgements

I would like to thank:

The publishing team at Footnote. Special thanks to Candida Lacey for believing in what was possible, Vicki Heath Silk for her keen eye, and Anna Morrison for the beautiful cover.

The editors of *The Smart Set*, *The Common*, and *SOFTBLOW*, where earlier versions of some of these poems and essays were first published.

John Schad for helping this book take its first steps in the world.

My father, Rodney, for his stories.

Chanda, Nicole, Kristi, and Sally for their friendship.

My husband, Cody, for his insights, for making me laugh, for wrangling the herd, for the unflagging encouragement, and for being my best friend.

About the author

Natasha Burge is a Saudi-born American writer whose family lived in the Arabian Gulf for more than half a century. She holds a PhD in creative writing and her work has been published around the world, anthologized, nominated for a Pushcart Prize, made a finalist for the Restless Books Prize for New Immigrant Writing and the Dzanc Prize for Fiction, and translated into Arabic, Mandarin, and Japanese.

FOOTNOTE

Footnote is a disruptive publisher focusing on migration, identity and marginalised knowledge and experience. We are committed to spotlighting previously overlooked or excluded ways of thinking, being and organising. Our mission is to counter dominant narratives and retell the story.

Our books span stimulating and politically engaged fiction and non-fiction, including history, current affairs, philosophy, memoir, reportage, climate, and more. Footnote launched in Spring 2022, in partnership with Bonnier Books UK.

Contact us for more information: **info@footnotepress.com**

Sign up to our mailing list at **footnotepress.com**

Follow us **@wearefootnote**

Voice of the Fish

Lars Horn

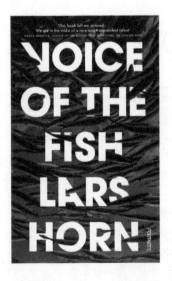

Lars Horn's kaleidoscopic, hallucinatory memoir explores the trans experience through meditations on aquatic life and mythology, and against the backdrop of travels in Russia and a debilitating injury that left the author temporarily unable to speak, read and write.

'*Voice of the Fish* is a mighty and innovative work . . . adventurous, bold, anti-authoritarian, and physical, we would all be well served to take note of this generation of new writers to which Horn belongs, sending us missives from the future of language and storytelling – more exacting, broad and excellent than we have yet imagined.' **Casey Legler**

'This book left me stunned. Breathtaking in its scope and generosity, it is at once a personal memoir and an examination of ancient worlds and marine life, and a luminous and compassionate reckoning with borders and boundaries. And all of this written in achingly beautiful prose that catches the light in even the darkest of moments. We are in the midst of a rare and transcendent talent.' **Maaza Mengiste**

Map of Hope and Sorrow

Helen Benedict and Eyad Awwadawnan

Award-winning Columbia University professor Helen Benedict teams up with Syrian writer Eyad Awwadawnan to present the stories of five refugees who have endured long and dangerous journeys from the Middle East and Africa to Greece.

These compelling, first-person stories of resilience, suffering and hope trace their journeys from Syria, Afghanistan, Nigeria and Cameroon to the brutal refugee camps, where they find themselves trapped in a strange and hostile world.

'Heartfelt, eye-opening, timely, essential.' **Christy Lefteri**

'Simple, powerful stories told in refugees' own voices. I couldn't stop reading, hand to mouth, my chest tightening.' **Dina Nayari**

'Harrowing, heartbreaking and deeply humane… Their voices echoed in my brain long after the final page.' **Jessica Bruder**

'This book celebrates human resilience and the capacity for hope, serving as a powerful call for tolerance.' ***The Observer***

All Else Failed: The Unlikely Volunteers at the Heart of the Migrant Aid Crisis

Dana Sachs

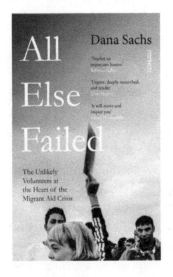

As hundreds of thousands of displaced people sought refuge in Europe, the global relief system failed. This is the story of the volunteers who stepped forward to help.

Dana Sachs's compelling eyewitness account weaves together the lives of seven individuals and their families – including a British coal miner's daughter, a Syrian mother of six, and a jill-of-all-trades from New Zealand – who became part of an extraordinary effort to care for their fellow humans.

'Dana Sachs's vivid, passionate book will move and inspire you, and bring a lump to your throat, by its portraits of big-hearted women and men from many countries who jumped in to help fellow human beings caught up in one of the worst humanitarian catastrophes of our time.' **Adam Hochschild**

'An urgent, deeply researched, and tender account of the helpers who arrive when those responsible for the chaos have turned their backs. Vital, and often infuriating, it is at once global in scale and absolutely singular.' **Dina Nayeri**

Living Together: Searching for Community in a Fractured World

Mim Skinner

Seventy-six per cent of people feel that we've become more distanced from our neighbours in the last twenty years. We are less likely than our grandparents, or even our parents, to know the names of our neighbours, to enjoy multi-generational friendships or to share resources and childcare. With mental health at epidemic levels, the climate crisis worsening, and society feeling increasingly divided, this game-changing book explores communities that have rejected individualism and nuclear family life in order to embrace a more collective way of living.

Mixing memories and reflections of her own unconventional upbringing with interviews and research into the international history of communalism, Mim Skinner challenges her own assumptions as well as ours as she searches for a more meaningful way of life and finds multiple options for alternative ways of living – from commercial co-living developments for time-starved urbanites to off-grid farm communities, low-cost co-operative estates and collaborative parenting schemes.

The result is an eye-opening snapshot of alternative communities and a much-needed new perspective on the concept of wellness.

Strong Female Character

Hanna Flint

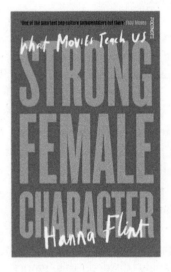

The leading film critic of her generation and staunch feminist of mixed-race heritage, Hanna Flint has succeeded in an industry not designed for people like her. Interweaving anecdotes from familial and personal experiences, she offers an eloquent, insightful and humorous reflection on the screen's representation of women and ethnic minorities, revealing how cinema has been the key to understanding herself, her body image and her ambitions as well as the world we live in.

Warm, funny and engaging and full of film-infused lessons, *Strong Female Character* will appeal to readers of all backgrounds and seeks to help us better see ourselves in our own eyes rather than letting others decide who and what we can be.

'One of the smartest pop culture commentators out there, Hanna is able to filter the latest releases through a sophisticated lens of social justice with wit and flair.' ***Guardian***

'At a time when fluff and gossip reign supreme, Hanna Flint's work is consistently insightful, informative and engaging all at once. I always finish reading it feeling just a tad bit smarter.' ***Huffington Post***